T0147570

AN ACCESSIBLE APPROACH TO OBTAIN WHOLENESS

The way is open unto all / A full joy

Elder G. E. Johnson

iUniverse, Inc.
New York   Bloomington

AN ACCESSIBLE APPROACH
TO OBTAIN WHOLENESS
The way is open unto all / A full joy

iUniverse books may be ordered through booksellers or by contacting:

iUniverse
1663 Liberty Drive
Bloomington, IN 47403
www.iuniverse.com
1-800-Authors (1-800-288-4677)

ISBN: 978-1-4401-1663-6 (pbk)
ISBN: 978-1-4401-1664-3 (ebk)

Printed in the United States of America

iUniverse rev. date: 3/17/09

This is not just a motivational or inspirational book
in the normal sense of the term.
But an on going, daily, spiritual process whose aim is
far greater than a trophy for the mantle.

Special Dedications ———————————

In loving memory

To my mother, Ms. Queen Ester Johnson: I am deeply grateful for the love and care of my mother, I cherish her memory. She truly was a gifted and dedicated person to her children, grandchildren, her church, and to anyone who was in need. My mother provided food for the hungry. She opened her home to other people's children and loved and cared for them as if they were her own. Due to circumstances beyond her control, my mother was left to care for her children on her own, but she was totally committed to providing and caring for us as no one else could have been. She was truly a Queen.

To my father, Mr. Will Johnson Sr.: For the little time he was with us, he was a good father, I am thankful for my dad. As a little boy, my brothers and I learned much from the teachings of our father.

To my younger sister, Floristean Johnson Wilson: She is greatly missed. I could always depend on her to help me with my schoolwork. We've had the most wonderful and enjoyable times together as a family. I truly miss her.

To my youngest brother, Sergeant Henry Alvin Johnson: My dear brother, you are deeply missed as well. So often I fall into pleasant memories of our childhood days. Even as adults, we shared so many happy occasions that will remain in my heart forever.

Acknowledgments ————————————

I don't think I could have written this book without the strong encouragement and support of my family and friends. To my sons Maurice Johnson, Donovan Johnson, Benjamin Johnson and Caleb Johnson, you all are a great inspiration to me, and also my beautiful and lovely daughters, Laketta R, Brazzle and Sheila E, Moffett. I am so pleased to be the one who God has blessed to be your father; I love you all very much. I never realized that being your dad could be so much fun. My grandchildren, I love you all very much.

I am particularly grateful to you Laketta, for your assistance in penning this book with the perfect title. I also am truly inspired by your first published book of beautiful poetry that you have written entitled "Ntouch."

Special love and thanks to my brothers and sisters: Deacon Jay Johnson, Ben Davis, Will Johnson Jr., Helen M. Burks and Ernestine Shanks, and also each and every one of my wonderful nieces and nephews. Thank you Jay, for when I came to you about writing this book you gave me much encouragement; it means so much to me to get that push from your big brother.

My deepest thanks go to my lovely and beloved wife Linda Johnson. Thanks for your patience with me while working on this project. Your loyalty and calm confidence kept me motivated as I was completing this manuscript to be published. You have listened to me and loved me through it all, and for that, I love you very much, and as the years come and go, I will love you even more.

I have become acutely aware of a truth so aptly stated by the poet John Donne, that " no man is an island," my family gives me great hope and inspiration… Family is the strongest institution there is; I love you all so dearly.

Acknowledgments

I owe a special debt of gratitude to two wonderful people, Ms. Inaz Deloney and Ms. Christine Fortune. I am particularly grateful for your support and your patience with me while working on this book. I truly appreciate the practical ideas and suggestions that you provided. I don't think I could have completed this book without your assistance.

Ms. Inaz Deloney of the Abundant Life Church Of God In Christ, I appreciate your wisdom and feedback and the understanding you showed toward what I was trying to put in writing. Your help has been outstanding.

Ms. Christine Fortune of the DeKalb County School system, I am deeply grateful to you for your ingenuity and tenacity. It would be remiss of me to think this book could have reached its full potential without your incredible vision and the personal guidance you provided. The diligence and attentive care you provided me while working on this book was invaluable. Although the words may be overused, "I can't thank you enough."

Finally, I truly thank God for the Christ like Spirit that is so obviously visible in the both of you. You were the ones all the time who were in His will to assist me in the writing of this book. May His choice blessing be yours.

Contents

Biblical Counseling For Healing of the Soul............1

Humanistic methods, psychotherapy, nor psychological techniques for cures cannot bring about spiritual healing.

Complete Success?….. Something is Missing!........11

People can be ever so rich with all of the material things of life and still be empty inside.

Faith to Keep Moving Forward 25

You must understand the devil doesn't want you to know that you are closer to your victory than you realize.

Life After the Fall...37

Faith will give us the assurance that we can turn our scars into stars, we can be better because of our brokenness, we are not alone, no we are never alone.

The Torment of Suffering:
You Don't Have to Give Up 55

We must always bear in mind that the same God who brought us through all of the other tribulations in the past, as painful as the present trials may be He is the one who will carry us through this with joy.

Foreword

This book comes at a crucial point and time in our lives. It comes at a time in the history of our church that we truly need to hear a word from God. It is time for the spiritual call of the real preacher man and woman to turn from humanistic methods of curing men's sin sick souls. The time is now to do a clarion call for man and woman to truly turn back to the great physician Himself for real spiritual healing.

We are in a spiritual warfare. Humanistic methods, psychotherapy, nor psychological techniques for cures cannot bring about spiritual healing. There must be a ringing cry of warning that our hope lies not in the ways of man, but in the propitious life and love of Jesus Christ Himself.

This book comes at a time in the history of the church that many of its pulpits are being occupied by predators in sheep's clothing (Matt.7: 15). They are pretending to speak for the Lord Himself while in reality speaking in favor of the world ways.

The message that you will receive from this book is clear in its counsel and direction; it come with sound and wise insights of the Spirit of the Lord. In the reading of it you should have a positive expectation and your faith in the power of God, as He will continually transform you into wholeness' as He would have you to be.

Therefore, the reading of this book should be required for all, and those who are entrusted with the care and soul of man. There may be someone you know, perhaps a friend or family member who is in need of spiritual healing from within. The purchase of this book, as a gift of love to them will provide ministry of wholeness.

Introduction ──────────────────

Much time and study has gone into the writing this book. It gives me great joy to present to you its pages. You will find it to be not only a most instructive, but also a most constructive view of life. You will be both encouraged and instructed in reading its contents. Many who are in the field of ministry may find the reading of this book to be an uncomfortable truth. However, it is the truth, and it is the truth that will make you free. As responsible individuals, it is my hope that you will derive a new understanding, revise in your thoughts, and change your behavior for the better, as you come to a renewed understanding of who you are in Christ by reading this book.

> *From the Holy Bible, we find these wonderful words as king David gives God praise for His marvelous works and the love of man.*

"O Lord, our Lord, how excellent is thy name in all the earth! Who hast set thy glory above the heavens. When I consider thy heavens, the work of thy fingers, and the stars, which thou hast ordained; what is man, that thou art mindful of him? And the son of man, that thou visitest him? For thou hast made him a little lower the angels, and hast crowned him with glory and honour. Thou madest him to have dominion over the works of thy hands; thou hast put all things under his feet: All sheep and oxen, yea, and the beasts of the field; the fowl of the air, and the fish of the seas. And whatsoever passeth through the paths of the seas. O Lord our Lord, how excellent is thy name in all the earth!" (Psa.8: 1,3-9)

Now these words that I am about to say, you may have heard them before, Notwithstanding I must now repeat them but only in serious reality; you see **we have a God who loves us so, so much that He gave His only begotten Son**

for us, that we may have life everlasting. How marvelous is the love of God. His love enables us to overcome sin and it's consequences, to live in relationship with Him, and to be transformed into the image of Christ.

There are three key principles that should stand out in the reading of this book. These three principles are: first, "As individuals we are responsible; second, as people we continually make choices in life; and third as being accountable, we should yield ourselves unto the Lord and allow Him to guide and direct us." You will realize in my discussion that it derives from several subject matters. Now in them I claim not to be an authority on any particular subject, But I have been given diligently to much study from the book of all books, from its pages the transformation of my understanding is sound in it's insight. And with more than twenty years as a pastor and spiritual guide, my associate degree is in theology and pastoral counseling.

Therefore by the grace of God I am what I am. His grace that is bestowed upon me is not in vain.

Chapter 1

Biblical Counseling For Healing of the Soul

We are experiencing a time in our lives like we have never before in the Christian community. So many of our small, storefront buildings are being replaced by large, extensive, mega buildings. From our TV sets and Internet, we are able to view live church services from around the world at the push of a button.

Today many of our churches have their own banks, and financial institutions. Many of these ministries are building homes, apartment buildings, schools and day care centers for their people and others. The list goes on. The progress of the church today is exciting. But yet, this is a crucial point and time for the church.

There are more and more people who attend church services today than in times past. Free transportation is provided to those who need it. Childcare is available during the time of church services to free mom/dad of any distractions. But in spite of all of the humanistic and materialistic progress and

1

advancements we have made in the Christian community, we are at a grievous time in the church ministry today.

In the 3rd Chapter of Second Timothy, the Apostle Paul foretells the wickedness of the last days. He says perilous (grievous) times shall come. Men shall have a form of Godliness, but denying the power thereof. They are ever learning, and never able to come to the knowledge of the truth. He continues his message in the 4th Chapter with a charge to Timothy to preach the word be instant in season, out of season; reprove, rebuke, exhort with all longsuffering and doctrine (teaching). For the time will come when they will not endure sound doctrine; but after their own lusts shall they heap to themselves teachers, having itching ears; and they shall turn away their ears from the truth, and shall be turned unto fables. And in the last part of the 5th verse of that 4th chapter, the Apostle Paul encourages Timothy to make full proof (fulfill) of his ministry.

My point here is this; out of all the progress that we have made and are making in our church ministry, **the soul of man is sin sick.** He has a problem in living and that is a problem that must be dealt with first as a spiritual problem with spiritual solutions. A change has to occur from within spiritually. God has created each of us with responsibility for choices. As people each of us have the ability to respond to God, we have the ability to respond to people, we have the ability to respond to thoughts and we have the ability to respond to life. Therefore biblical counseling is necessary and is the only true method for change in the right direction.

At the present time I acknowledge that in today's church, man has benefited very well; the advancements and achievements to better him are incredible. By and large, numerous of these ministries are teaching men and women how to start up their own business and to buy their own homes. There are single classes for men and women on how to find a good wife or husband, men night out and a day off for mother. These ministries are marvelous in so many ways. The people are well informed and have acquired many skills for the work place.

But at the same time, I don't think we should be so eager in our endeavor with our various programs in ministry such as psychological techniques, ministry of prosperity and others, that we forget the essence of ministry. Then there are other useful ministries of materialism that causes many of us to forget the true purpose in calling. When true essence of purpose is misunderstood the people become mislead. They receive the thought that these useful programs have greater emphasis and a more importance in value than the needful ministry for a spiritual change from within. When the souls of the people are being misled in their understanding from the pulpits, we are defeating the purpose of the true essence in church ministry.

As previously stated we give much credit to the various ministries and we are truly grateful for the good that they are doing. But is this the **essence** of church ministry? Or **the true character** in which the church consist? It is very clear that so many of our people who come to these church services in this day and time have one goal in mind and that is to acquire knowledge on how to become financially and generally successful in life. Most of these people who attend these church services they have very little concern for their own soul if any at all. They are there to hear and receive a message on the teachings of prosperity. For the most part many of these people are not attending these church services in large numbers to hear the preached word concerning the blood of Jesus. But rather they are there to hear the teachings of prosperity or some other gospel.

The preaching on the blood of Jesus'
Should not be secondary

Now the teachings on prosperity are not wrong in it self. I do know and understand that it does have its place in ministry. Many of our people have benefited very much from this kind of ministry. We do realize the teachings on prosperity have empowered many of our people in life and even in ministry. But when we pimp the Cross at the mercy of prosperity, the soul of the people have been shortchanged. The blood of Jesus' should not be used as a by-product (secondary) in ministry. Our most highest emphasis in ministry should be on the preaching and teachings of the blood of Jesus Christ. The most significance and ultimate concern and reason that anyone should have for attending church services should be for the concern of their own soul.

The most absolute fact we must realize is that everyday we are leaving from this earth. All of the stuff we have accumulated is being left behind. We must then stand before God Himself to give in account of our soul.

Jesus asked, this question in Matt.16: 26. For what is a man profited, if he shall gain the whole world, and lose (forfeit) his own soul? Or what shall a man give in exchange for his soul? The point to be made here is that when we don't truly know Christ, we make choices as though this life is all we have. In reality, this life is just the introduction to eternity. The way in which we live this brief span of life here on earth however will, determines our eternal state. All of the material gains we accumulate on earth have no value in purchasing eternal life. The highest social or civic honors that we can achieve here on earth cannot earn our way into heaven.

Christ is concerned about our physical and spiritual needs. Here we find in Third John Chapter 1;2, in John's writing to Gaius (a prominent Christian in the early church.) He says beloved, I wish above all things that thou mayest prosper and be in health, even as thy soul prospereth. Christ is concerned for both body and soul. He wants us to live a good life but also to be accountable unto Him. As responsible Christians, we should never be so indulgent in worldly gains that we neglect the need for our soul.

From Luke 12:16-20, as Christ comes near the end of one of His many parables, He is speaking with His disciples, He warns them against the neglect of the soul. By giving this stunning statement: (Thou fool, this night thy soul shall be required of thee.) In this He tell them of a certain rich man whose ground had brought forth abundance. The rich man said within himself I have no room to bestow all of my goods. This will I do. I will pull down my barns and build greater (bigger) barns. There I will bestow all of my goods, and I will say to my soul, Soul thou hast much goods laid up for many years. Take thine ease, eat. Drink, and be merry.

But God's reply to him was, "Thou fool this night thou soul is required of thee. Then whose shall those things be, which thou hast provided?" He continues, "and so is he that layeth up treasure for himself, and is not rich toward God." When one is rich with this worlds goods and not rich toward God, the question remains, what is a man profited, if he shall gain the whole world, and lose his soul? Now, for your consideration, when you truly evaluate all that happens from an eternal perspective, you will find your values and decisions changing.

How can any one be so blind, or so dumb, as to go through life, and face death, without their soul being at peace with God? In Eze.18: 4, the Word of the Lord says, Behold, all souls are mine; as the soul of the Father, so also of the son is mine: the soul that sinneth, it shall die. We all have to die (natural death), and it is something that you can't play off. Apart from Christ, what is there, to make life worthwhile, either in this world or the next? Christ, He is the center and heart of the bible. He is the center and heart of history, and

Jesus Christ should be the center and heart of our lives. Our Eternal Destiny is in His hand. Our Acceptance or Rejection of Him will determine for each of us Eternal Glory in Heaven with Him, or Eternal Damnation in Hell. In Hell it is a place where we will be separated from the love of God. It is either one or the other.

The most important decision any one could ever be called upon to make in his or her heart is to accept Christ into their life. To accept Christ as Savior, Lord and Master to strive sincerely and devotedly to follow in the way and the life of Him in which He taught. This is the only **true cure for the soul** of man. It is the most Glorious thing any one can do which is to be save, and to live a holy life, it is the most exalted privilege of mankind. It is the most satisfactory way of life. In Rev. 3:20, we have these words of Christ, "Behold I stand at the door: and knock; if any man hear my voice, and open the door, I will come in to him and will sup with him and he with me." When one finds that peace with God he has a new out look on life. This means he has peace of mind, contentment of heart, forgiveness, happiness, hope, life abundant, and life that shall never end.

A POWER SHORTAGE

For those of you who have turned back and have gone into a different direction, away from the cross, I appeal to you to return unto the Lord before it is too late. I am so proud of all of the true man and woman of God, those of you who are standing strong, and are faithfully committed to this Holy walk of faith. I encourage those of you as well as you who are preaching and teaching the word of God, to do so without wavering, or compromising. I Thank God for you my brothers and sisters. While many are falling by the way side by compromising the word of God for selfish and materialistic gains, you all are standing strong. You are steadfast, and determined in doing the will of the Lord in these last and evil days. You are the true heroes of faith. Keep up the good work. And having said that, it brings me to my next point.

"There is a power shortage in the church, now the power shortage is not in the lighting that illuminates the buildings. Nor is it in the support beams that hold the structure of the building together. No, This is not the kind of shortage I am speaking of. It is not a materialistic, or humanistic kind of power that is lacking in the church. The power shortage that we are experiencing is a Spiritual one. There can be no substitute for it.

There are many things that can be replaced in the church, but the Holy Spirit of God is not one of them. So that no one will misunderstand the point in my endeavor, I am speaking of the power of the Holy Ghost, (the comforter). Jesus said the Holy Ghost, who is the Spirit of truth, whom He would send from the Father, He is to abide in you, He will teach, lead and guide you into all truth. In Acts the 1st chapter, verse 8, Christ give this declared statement; But ye shall receive power, after that the Holy Ghost is come upon you. When one is trying to lead the church without the power of the Holy Ghost he is only giving room for the spirit of darkness to take place. This is a deceiving spirit of Satan, and when this spirit takes place in the church it becomes a playground for the works of the devil.

It is very sad, the time in which we live to see so many of our people unspiritual fulfilled who are going to church each Sunday but their soul is crying in hunger for the word of God. These people are in need of spiritual healing. They are people who are hurting, broken, sick, confused. They are people who are experiencing trouble in their marriage, and those who are experiencing troubles of other kinds. There are others who are experiencing the torments of demons and need to be set free. For the most part these people are unable to receive the spiritual help that they desire, and truly need in order to be set free or delivered. There is a spiritual deficiency in many of our churches today, because so many of its pulpits are being occupied by leaders who do not have the soul of the people at heart.

They are leaders who have a form of Godliness but denying the power thereof. For they have a form of Godliness, but no power. Now I must say that on any given Sunday one can find good entertainment, and it may gratify him to the fullest degree but it can only satisfy the humanistic part of him. The soul is the spiritual part of man.

Humanistic methods of entertainment can't bring about deliverance for a man's soul. The soul of man is hungering and thirsting after (righteousness) salvation. This can come only through the preach word of God, in demonstrations of the Holy Ghost, and with power. Enticing words of man's wisdom does not do anything for the soul of man.

HE IS KNOCKING.

One should never be so busy enjoying worldly pleasures that they can't hear Christ trying to enter. The pleasures of this world-----money, material possessions, can be an interposing barrier because their temporary satisfaction makes one indifferent to God's offer of lasting satisfaction. Letting Him in is the only hope of lasting fulfillment. Christ is knocking at the door of our heart, He wants to have fellowship with us, and that we will open up to Him. He is patient and persistent in trying to get through to us, but not by breaking in to enter, but knocking, allowing us to decide whether or not to open up our lives to Him.

As we open up our lives to Christ for Him to live inside of us and we in Him, we will then have fellowship with Him, "God's Son." That means we are now no longer walking in darkness, but we are walking in the light as He is in the light. Light represents what is good, pure, true, holy and reliable.

Darkness represents sin and evil. "God is light". He is perfectly holy and true. He alone can guide us out of the darkness of sin. Sin, by its very nature, brings death. The bible tells us in Romans 6:23. For the wages of sin is death; but the gift of God is eternal life through Jesus Christ our Lord. You see we are free to choose between two masters, but we are not free to adjust the consequences of our choice. If we want to have a relationship with Christ, we must put aside our sinful ways of living, and accept Him as our lord and savior.

I firmly believe that in biblical counseling when the love of God is ministered in a balance of mercy and truth it provide both a supportive environment and direction for change.

Chapter 2

Complete Success?…..
Something is Missing!

As a little boy growing up in Mississippi, I thought complete success and happiness was to be rich, have a big beautiful home, and to own a big black expensive car (preferably a Lincoln) like the one I would see on T.V. the car that the president of the united states rode in. This is what I thought complete success and happiness would be for me or any one else, who would achieve that level in life. I thought to myself, what else in life could there be better? If any one who was rich and famous, with a big beautiful home and owned an expensive car, (preferably a Lincoln) I thought that was the kind of life that was truly worth living.

Then later in my young life as I was growing up, I would see the strangest thing that would be playing out on T.V. It was so surprising and astonishing that it was hard for me to believe at first. This is what was so perplexing to me; the perplexing thing I saw back then was rich and famous people committing suicide. These were people who seemed to have everything that any one could ever wish for in this life. Why would they end their own life? What could cause a person who seem to have everything any one could ever whish for, to have a need to end their life? These people would intentionally kill themselves by jumping off a building, taking a gun and shooting themselves in the head, taking an overdose in pills, or committing some other destructive manner to end their life. These reports were very disturbing to me.

Then the next thing that was so astonishing and perplexing was that sometime they would leave a note or letter behind for others to read. In general which could be summed up that they felt they had nothing in life to live for. It amazed me to see people who seem to have everything that would make life worthwhile, to hear them say that there is a void in their life, and for that reason they have no inner peace.

In my growing up as a young man, I came to the understanding and the conclusion that people can be ever so rich with all of the material things of life and still be empty inside. Now don't misunderstand me, it is a blessing for any of us to be rich financially and with much goods. We then have the opportunity to be a great blessing in kingdom work, and helping others. But my concern is this; I must say that I am convinced, that no one can ever truly have inner peace apart from Jesus Christ. It is required of us all to love the Lord with all of our heart, soul, mind and strength. The only true way we can ever have inner peace within, is to allow Christ to be the center and Lord of our life. Without inner peace, your spirit is tormented because only Christ can fulfill that void within your life.

We all should strive to do our best in life: in our community, in the work place, and provide the best of care for our families, doing this is no more than we should do. You see to do these things is required of us all as responsible adults; it is what I call necessary living. It is also necessary that we all should live a purposeful life. To live a life of purpose, which is intentional living, a life that is accountable unto Christ. The understanding that we should have in this life is that we all are accountable unto Christ. We are not our own. We do not live unto our self. We depend on Him for our very life.

We've all has seen or know those people who have the "average" job, earning the " average" income. However, most of those same people have the latest and greatest big screen t.v, cell phones, the biggest house on the block and the best of cars in the driveway. They appear to be very successful and happy when you see them.

The reality of these people is they are living from check to check to check. The only problem with that is their check never really covers their bills. They are often late making their payments, receiving repo notices of their car and threats of foreclosure the mortgage of their house. Yet they put a fake smile on their face and act like nothing is wrong. Inside money is a huge issue at the dinner table. Money is a huge concern and they are always wondering how that next payment will be made. Living beyond your means can be a huge gamble, one wrong move or missed payment and you could lose it all.

Each of us should want to do well in life and be prosperous. As we allow these opportunities to presents themselves we should also be accountable as well as living a responsible life. We each have our part in making this world a better place to live in. It does not make any difference whether we are rich or poor. We are to live responsible lives. Now having said that, it brings me to my next point which is this: so many people are lost with the idea of a life style they are living that is too costly for them in more ways than they realize. It is a life style that is apart from purpose. Their utmost concern is materialism rather than accountability or responsibility. These are people who are perpetrating. So many of them are living from paycheck to pay check. Their money is owed out before they ever get it. These people who I call perpetrators are the ones who are living large on a food stamp income.

Now to those of you who are living large and can afford the life style that you are living, you are blessed. You are blessed as you live wisely, responsibly, and accountably. You have the opportunity to give more into kingdom ministry to help further the gospel. Further, you are blessed to be a blessing in other areas that are wanting. You who can afford to live the life style must live it responsible.

Perpetrators are the kind of people who live beyond their means. They wear name brand clothing, drives big SUV trucks but can't afford to keep gas in it or keep up the note on it as well, nor pay for the care of their children. These are those who are living on a food stamp income they buy $200.00 tennis shoes for their kid's feet but can't buy food for them to eat or pay their rent. These kinds of people are lost in the idea of buying a $60.000 car but don't know how to buy an affordable house to put their family in. They are lost in the mindset of what true success is all about.

It is so dismal to see how so many people who are driven with the **thought of success**. We find it here in this country more than any other. The mindset of materialism seems to be the utmost concern. Their thought is that you must have the biggest house on the block to show your success, and drive an expensive car which most of them cannot afford. Then they buy into the idea that you must wear expensive, top of the line, name brand clothing. There is the high cost of furniture in the house that they can hardly pay for. Please don't misunderstand me this is all well and good if you can afford these things. My concern is for those who can't afford to be in the race of material gain and allow greater needs and concerns to be neglected. Of course who would dare go out in public without wearing some high-priced jewelry? Any one less than this are looked down on as not being much, or too poor to keep up.

Many of our church ministries are playing into this philosophy of materialism. There are pastors who will preach to the people "the gospel of prosperity" but very little gospel concerning "**The Blood of Jesus.**" Many of these ministers are preaching this "have all" ministry of success to the people, but fail to tell them that Christ must be first in their lives. A great number of these kind of ministries are telling the people that if they don't have the big money, the big nice home, drive an expensive car they are not bless. They are also saying if you are not wearing all of the name brand clothes, or have the costly jewelry, then you are not being bless by God. It is a shame that so many of our people are driven with this "thought of success" that they see the church as a place to seek for riches, rather than Christ Himself. The Bible tells us in (I must repeat it again) Matt.6: 33 "But seek ye first the kingdom of God, and his righteousness; and all these things shall be added unto you."

Any one who sees the church only as a place to seek the teaching of prosperity has no true fellowship with Christ. The fact is this: people who only see God as someone, or something that they can pray to and to get stuff or material gain from, they have no true commitment with the Father.

People are so hung up on the thought of keeping up with the Jones. If the Jones buys a new car, then we must buy a new car as or more expensive one than the Jones. If the Jones put a swimming pool in their back yard, we must now put a swimming pool in our back yard. They carelessly buy into this game of competing with the Jones whether they can afford to or not. In all fairness very few of them can. A friend who is a real estate broker with his own realty company, he and I was talking one day on this same subject. I ask him what would be his point of view on the subject of people trying to compete with each other? His reply to my was, "Well Mr. J, people feel good just to show off to their friends and the public that they are living large. It is a costly game but they are going to do it any way, much of my business come from people who buy what they can't afford."

I asked him to explain what he meant by that comment. He replied by saying "Mr. J, you know our parents taught us years ago that we should save earnestly and spend wisely. People could have more, and own more, but the process is too slow for them, they want it now at any cost." He continues, "for example I can sell a couple a very nice home that is within their budget, but they would rather buy a home that cost far more than they can afford just to appear to be more successful than they really are. Thereby the sacrifices that now comes into play at the expense of neglect. These sacrifices can be that of our family, our health, seeking the will of God, and other concerns and matters of importance that should not go undone."

As he continued: "The down side to this is now that they are living outside of their budget, they have to take on a second job. They are more stressed than before by trying to keep up. The additional problem is that the higher cost in bills are now coming in, they are now paying out more and their stress level is higher. When one is stressed out it can cause problems in their relationships as well as with their health. Stress is what happens when you feel that your demands go beyond your resources, and it is so important for them to pay attention to the warning signals of stress. And believe it or not, 35% of these people will lose their house within three to five years." He ended his statement by saying: "If people would live within their means, and invest smart, they can live better, have more, and own more." The important message one can receive from this is the needless sacrifices in trying to keeping up with the Jones can produce neglect, and true concerns go unattended.

A high school teacher whom I have known for many years he and his wife both taught in public school. Both of these people worked very hard having two full time jobs. His second job was working in a factory. He would often say to me the reason both of them (he and his wife) worked as hard as they do is because they do not want their kids to ever want for nothing. It seem like they would buy their kids every thing they wanted. His day of work would begin at 7:am each morning and end at 11:pm that night five days a week, and sometime on Saturdays. His wife workweek was about the same as his. I remember many times he would be found sleeping in school during the class period. He seemed to never have enough rest. He and his wife did not have time for each other nor was there much time for the two children who also attended private school. There was very little time for God.

This family attended the same church on some Sunday mornings (when they were able to get up on time) where my family worshiped. Sadly to say, a few years later this high school teacher died at the age of 48, or 49 years old of a heart condition, and a year later his wife died of cancer. They owned a nice big beautiful home that was paid off by the insurance for the kids to enjoy, and there was a little money in the bank that was left for them also. Regretfully to inform you, in less than six months time the life of these two young adults started going down hill. Within one year they lost the home that their father and mother worked so hard for. And the money that was in the bank their parents left behind for them was all gone in a very short time. All of their substance was wasted in a very short while due to their riotous living.

This young man and young lady mom and dad had given all of their time on jobs working to give them a good life. But after the death of their mom and dad, these two young adults have spent most of their adult life in and out of jail because of their involvement in drugs and other unlawful acts. It has been some years past but the last report that I did receive of them, the young man who would be now about forty, or forty one years old has been in prison for many years. His sister who is now about thirty-nine years old, is living from one homeless shelter to another, and in the streets due to her continual uses of drugs. There is still hope for these two young people and my prayer is that they will find that peace with God in time.

Now I am not saying every case as this is the same or will turn out this way when one has on time for their family due to the fact they are so involved in the drive for success. But it is surely not a good thing to do, be sure that there is quality time spent with family. There must be some time for family, and God. When anyone abandons their family just to be free to work all day and most of the night, so that their family will never need for anything, I think they fail to understand "some me time." No one must ever get so involved in the cares of wanting so much in this life of materialism that they neglect their love ones in the process. My next point is this: we must never get so entangled in the cares of this world that we fail to honor God by living a responsible life unto him. It is He who has made us and not we ourselves; He must be the center of our lives.

Life is what you make of it. In so many ways this is very true, but are we going at it the right way? You see you and I can decide to a large degree what our life will be by the decisions we make. You can decide yourself into failure or into success. Now let me make this very clear. When I speak of success I am not speaking of just having wealth, to say one who is very rich with more money than he or she will ever need. No, this is not the kind of success I am speaking of. We should do our best in providing and caring for our family and love ones, with Christ being the center of our will. The success I am speaking of is wholeness. I firmly believe we should strive to be successful in the righteousness of God. For the bible tells us in (Matt.6: 33:) "But seek ye first the Kingdom of God, and his righteousness; and all these things shall be added unto you." "Nothing broken, nothing missing" what am I saying here? Well, I am speaking of wholeness. In order for one to have a truly successful life there must be wholeness.

One can be very rich in this world with money and all the find things of life and yet is empty inside. These things and the stuff that we own cannot give us inner peace that comes from God. Only He can make us whole. I believe that for anyone to be whole, and truly have a life that is successful in this world, it begins with seeking the kingdom of God and His righteousness.

It is not by how much money one may have. Notwithstanding, we all need money. It provides for our earthly needs, but money alone does not mean that we will be successful in every area of our life. If a man who is very wealthy and he is in a mental hospital because he has lost his mind he is no better off mentally, than a poor man in the same condition. They both have lost the uses of their mind. If a rich man is dying with cancer can his wealth stop him from dying? Life without Christ is one of darkness and obscurity. It means so much to have fellowship with Christ and a life that is being lived in relationship with him.

Life is fill with all manner of suffering and difficulty. It does not make any difference if you are rich or poor. From time to time life will throw some surprises your way and you are going to have your share of sorrow. Ready or not, life will introduce itself to you in various forms and from many sides. Sorrows are going to come in all of our lives at one time or another.

Therefore, it is so important to have a secure foundation in life, and that can only be found in Jesus Christ. If by chance you don't know Him, let me tell you a little about Him. He is a friend that will be closer to you than any brother. What I love about Him is he will not forsake you in time of trouble, sickness, or any other ills in life that will come your way. Jesus will give you hope in time of despair, joy in sorrow, strength in weakness. There is not a friend like Jesus: no, not one! He is a burden bearer and one who will supply all of your needs. Jesus Christ, and only Jesus Christ is the secure foundation for life ills. If you put your trust in Him, he will give you an abundant, and complete life.

It is foolish for any one to think that they can be secure, free and safe from all of life's ills by trusting in their wealth, or their own self worth. It is foolish of any man or woman to think that they have no need for God in their lives. Do you not know that we rely on God's faithfulness for the very air we breaths? Let us take a look at a verse in the Bible that I need to bring to your attention at this time, it is found in Rev.3: 17, "Because thou sayest, I am rich, and increased with goods, and have need of nothing; and knowest not that thou are wretched, and miserable, and poor, and blind, and naked." God who has made us. He knows all about us. He sees what we don't, and can't see, we don't know about tomorrow, but He holds tomorrow, all things, and time is in his hand. God created the heavens and earth, all things visible and invisible, thrones, dominions, principalities, or powers. All things were created by him and do consist.

The Bible says that God, our heavenly father has a plan for each of our individual lives. To fulfill that plan is nothing less than ultimate success in life. The more we allow the Lord to lead us into His plan for our lives, the more He is able to bless us physically, emotionally and spiritually. It all begins when we receive His love and begin to return His love. What we will realize is that out of the relationship that follows, we can go from some blessing to abundant blessing, but we must not fail to receive God's love. Receiving God's love is the key to knowing God personally and the key to receiving His abundant blessings of success in life

The essence of salvation is God's forgiveness, which is also the love of God. When we receive His love, we receive Him because He is love (1 john 4:8). When we receive Him, we can become victorious over sin. Jesus Christ, who is the Son of God paid the price for our sin with His life, but that was not the end of it, He was raised up (resurrected) by the power of the Holy Spirit. With His death, forgiveness of sin became available to anyone who asks for it with a repentant heart. Jesus death on the cross and His resurrected life from the grave provide us complete victory over all sin as we receive Him and continue in His love to obey His word, as we forgive others their trespasses.

Total knowledge

When we consider the omniscience of God, how secure are we without Him? What part of our success apart from God are we safe? Can we see the invisible? He has total knowledge knowing everything. There is nothing that is hid from him. The darkness is as day. He knows our thoughts afar off, even the secret things are revealed before him. The sickness, troubles, and sorrows that could be drawing near your direction even at this moment, that has not been manifested unto you yet, is known by the infinitely wise and all knowing God.

There are people who feel that they have done things in secret that no one knows about. I need to inform you, God knows all of our secret thoughts and actions. Every deed we have ever done, or will do is open and revealed before the presence of God. From the Holy Bible we will find the reading of His word; (Ecclesiastes 12: 13-14) "Let us hear the conclusion of the whole matter: Fear God, and keep his commandments: for this the whole duty of man. For God shall bring every work into judgment, with every secret thing, whether it be good, or whether it be evil." Therefore, God who knows all, sees all, and hears all before it ever comes into thought. It is He to whom no secret thing can be hid from the knowing of Him.

The presence of God

He is God omnipresent, the fact of being present everywhere at the same time, "God is so" and no one can ever be lost from the spirit of God. Here we have David who seeks his own personal conclusion of the presence of God, in the book of psalms 139: 7-12 (nkjv): "Where can I go from your spirit? Or where can I flee from your presence? If I ascend into heaven, you are there; if I make my bed in hell, behold, you are there. If take the wings of the morning, and dwell in the uttermost parts of the sea, even there your hand shall hold me. If I say, surely the darkness shall fall on me, even the night shall be light about me; indeed, the darkness shall not hide from you, but the night shines as the day; the darkness and the light are both alike to you." The point to be made here is, no matter what we do or where we go, we can never be far from God's comforting presence.

His unlimited power

There is no power but that of God, for He is omnipotent. God have all power, all authority, and force. He is unlimited in his power. He is the God of all creation; therefore we are accountable to live a responsible life onto Him. It is He who has made us and not we ourselves. Now to the point of living a morally good life, and have not received Christ in our lives our good is not good enough. We are guilty of the sin of omission: Failure to do what is required of us, which is to receive Christ as our Lord and savior. For any one to live a morally good live apart foam Christ has failed. We are required to live a life that is responsible unto him. My question is; how can any one feel safe and secure from God, by living in their wealth, success, or self worth, when at this very moment his life is in the hands of an all-powerful God?

Life after death

God is not one who keeps people guessing about who he is or what he expects of us. God is worshiped and served by true Christians. He reveals himself and his commandments to his people. We are responsible to respond to God's redemptive revelation and to turn from all sin and other gods. We must worship and serve Him and Him alone. Many people try to do good by being honest and doing what they feel is right, but Jesus said the only true way to live a truly good life is to stay in him and he in you. As a branch is attached to the vine, so are we in Him.

You see we must understand that this life that we now live in the flesh, is going to come to an end. Our lives here on this earth are temporal. This body that we live in is "mortal." The understanding of the word is, "man a being who must die." Therefore death is appointed unto every one, but death is not our final destination. It is a place and time of judgment by God to judge us for the things we have done, or have not done here on earth. It has been given, and is given by God through His word how we are to live here on this earth. The kind of life that "we make a choice to live" will be, and is before God to judge.

Jesus tells us that in order for us to have fellowship with Him we must abide in Him, and His word (He) abide in us. There is a strong warning that comes to us from the word of God in

Heb.9: 27, "And as it is appointed unto man once to die, but after this the judgment." Death cannot be escape by anyone. It is the common lot of all. A true fact everyone must understand this; "that is life after death." After our earthly body have gone back to the dust from which it came, and our spirit will return back to God who gave it: Then we shall all stand before the judgment seat of God, to give in account of our deeds. There is no way of getting around it

It is God who is going to judge us all for every deed we have done in our bodies whether they be good or bad. No one can escape from the presence of God. The Bible tells us how God made man (created him). It tells us that God made man from the dust of the earth, and breathed into his nostrils the "breath of life" and man became a "living soul." (Gen.2: 7). Thereby we are accountable unto God Therefore with the understanding that death is a common lot of us all, that no one cannot escape, the Bible also tells us in (Ecclesiastes 12: 7) "Then shall the dust return to the earth as it was: and the spirit shall return unto God who gave it." Now I come to my question and it is this: how can we have true success in this life apart from a true fellowship with our maker? It is going to be very disappointing for many of us on that day. Therefore we should not wait until that final day to find out what is missing. It will be too late.

CHAPTER 3

FAITH TO KEEP MOVING FORWARD

As we walk this walk of faith we must be steadfast and determine in our faith, because your adversary the devil is somewhere near by waiting to try and deprive you of your faith. His will in every step is to causes us to stumble and fall, give up altogether, or seek some other alternative walk. For this reason we face encounters, frustrations, obstacles, and other kinds of discouragements. Satan desires to deprive you of your joy. Therefore the bible tells us in (1 peter 5:8) "Be sober, be vigilant; because your adversary the devil, as a roaring lion, walketh about, and seeking whom he may devour." His will is to destroy your faith. He wants you to turn back from your walk with God and quit. But what should our determination be? It should be to keep moving forward and striving until we have climbed over, to find a way to pass through, to go around, to tunnel underneath, or simply to turn your mountain into a blessing.

As believers we are expecting to be victorious in our walk of faith knowing God who is able to see us through any and all of our problems. It is so encouraging to know that here is no problem that is too hard for God. When you have gone as for as you can go in doing your best in those things that are right, you then allow the Lord to help you the rest of the way. Know that He is present to help you through every step of the way. What is so comforting to know is this; He will not suffer you to be tempted above that you are able to endure. From his holy word; (1 Peter 5:7) "Casting all your care upon Him; for He careth for you." Yes, You can make it! There is no need to give up. Whatever troubles or hindrances you may be experiencing at this time and moment in your life it will pass. If you put your trust in Jesus everything will work out for the good. Your faith will see you through.

The Lord is concerned about His people. He will not leave you alone; you are not in this by yourself. Jesus said if I be for you I am more than the world against you. Again, He careth for you, it is so encouraging to know that we have such a loving and caring God who cares for us. How marvelous it is to have such a wonderful and loving God on your side, one who careth about your every concern.

When things appear to be so hard in your life, what do you do? When you are at that place of fear and uncertainties and you just don't know what to do or where to turn, just what do you do? Here is my answer to the question, just turn it over to Jesus. He is waiting to help you. The Lord is a way maker. There is this confirmation that says, He is a problem solver, a burden bearer, a heart fixer, and mind regulator. The troubles and torments that you may be suffering with may have you walking the floor all night long, not being able to sleep, but if you put it in the hands of the Lord he will fix it for you. "I've been there" but through it all I have learned to trust in Jesus and I have learned to trust in His word. Let me tell you, if you put your trust in Him, He will bring you out.

I am not telling you something that someone has told me; but to inform you I know Him for myself. I am speaking to you from personal experiences. There were times in my life that I thought I was not going to make it. But every time I turned my troubles over to the Lord and put them in His hands He would work it out for me. Each time I came out of that situation with victory. We must understand the God who we serve never fails, therefore with confidence we can build up ourselves on our most holy faith.

Now Satan will try to deceive you through your troubles. If you let him, he will have you to believe that if God does not fix your situation at the time you think he should that the Lord has failed you. You must know the devil is a lie. God cannot fail. The Lord will deliver His people. Do you have the faith to believe? His ears are open unto our cry and He knows just what we need, if you call on Him, God will answer prayer. I remember back as a little kid coming up, I would always hear my mother say; "**now you just have to trust the Lord, He may not come when you want Him to but, He will be on time.**" Those words I still keep in my spirit to this day. They have been strength to me at low times in my life.

I can tell you from my many years of personal experiences with the Lord that He will not fail you. Even when you come to those low trying times in your life that we all will encounter, that place where you feel like you just can't go any further, be encouraged you can make it. Know that the Lord is there to help you. Turn your situation over to Jesus. He is there to help you through your every care. There is no need to throw in the towel. You don't have to give up, you can make it, and your faith will bring you through.

We all have to go through some things sometime, but know this: we are stronger when we come out of our trials than we are before we go into them. You must understand the devil doesn't want you to know that you are closer to your victory than you realize. He doesn't want you to see the blessings that you are coming into. You must know that Satan is a deceiver, and I want you to also know that you are blessed. You have the victory. It is yours just receive it. It is deplorable to see so many people, who are standing at the door of their victory, but they will allow the devil to deceive them and give up, rather than to step over into their blessings. Don't give up! Your victory is at hand.

Putting your faith to
Work for you

Allow me to share with you these examples of "faith at work." Just recently, (April, 2008) my wife and I had gone to the store to purchase a few food supplies for a late night snack. Upon arriving at the store my wife decided to stay inside the car while I go in and get the supplies. After I had completed my shopping and had paid the cashier for the food items and was about to go out of the store without any warning, a very bad tornado was headed toward the grocery store. People was running back into the store horrified and very fearful of the storm, my concern at this time was the safety of my wife, I did not see her come inside the store with everyone else. So I ran outside to get her. By the time I had made it to my car to get my wife and bring her back into the store for safety from the storm, it was to late, the tornado had hit the grown. It was the most alarming and terrifying sound I think I have ever heard.

It was now too dangerous for us to try and make a run back into the store, neither was there no other place in the immediate area we could have ran to for safety from the storm. So I made the decision to get into the car (I am not advising anyone to use a car for safety from a tornado) with my wife to wait out the storm there. As we were waiting for it to pass over, I began to speak some comforting words of faith to her because she was very frightened which is understandable. As my wife and I were sitting in the car we were at peace with our trust in the Lord, knowing that He would take care of us. Although the tornado was very destructive to much of what was in its path, my wife and I were safe. It was so amazing; Regardless of how violent the storm was, as the debris that was caused by it was whirling all around us, we were safe in the hands of the Lord. The tornado pulled up a very large tree from the ground and it fell onto a house, cars were being moved all around us and several of them was damaged very bad. And the store that I came out of, part of the roof was taken off of it along with the ac units.

Note: A tornado is a characteristically dangers storm, which is very dangerous and deadly.
It is capable of destruction of any thing in its path, having the potential of causing many deaths. So in the event of such a storm, please seek shelter immediately

This was a horrific experience for my wife and me, we were in the mist of all of that destruction but God was then, and is now faithful. In spite of the danger that was happening at the time, which was caused by the tornado, the Lord had taken good care of my wife and me. The whirling wind was so strong that it was moving the other cars around as the alarms were sounding off on them, and as stated some was damaged very bad. During this experience, it was so astonishing for me to see Lord at work, He did not allow the whirling wind to move our car at all; my wife and I did not feel any movement of our car from the storm.

We were safe in the hands of the Lord. As we were sitting there in our car waiting for the tornado to pass over, our faith and trust was in Him who hold the power of the world in His hands. Therefore you should be encouraged to know that your faith in the Lord will be a covering to you from the storms of life. I am reminded of psalms 46:10a. "Be still, and know that I am God." When I look back over the years of my life, it is amazing how God has keep me, the Lord have keep me through the seen and the unseen dangers. I can truly say that I am blessed and highly favored of the Lord, because down through the years the He has taken good care of me.

Speaking of faith at work there was a house that I purchased many years ago for its historical value. I loved that house. It was a nice two-story home in a good area of the city. Now the Lord has blessed me in my being there in that area and I was a blessing to that community as well. Two years after being in my home, I had to move out of it due to some under ground problems. It was needful for me to move as soon as I could. Much of my money was put into this house in the form of a large cash down payment, and adding an addition on to the house and other repairs. This all added up to a large amount of my person money that was paid out. Only two years had passed and I had to vacate my home. It was very difficult for me. I had not had enough time to recover from these losses.

I began to look for another home and time was not on my side, I had to move very soon. I found out that when you are in a hurry, problems seem to arrive from every place. Now with little cash money to work with, it was not so easy to find the kind of home that I was looking for. I had experienced some difficult circumstances in trying to find a house right a way. At times it seem like nothing was working out right for me.

After much delay I finally found the house that I really wanted but I did not have the required amount of cash down payment. As I was standing there in the house talking with the owner of the property, there was this guy from an investment company that was there also to purchase the house for investment purposes. He said to me he would help me out by buying the house from the owner and selling it to me for a fair price. My reply to him was no that would be ok. Then I stated to him I will seek the Lord concerning my situation and see what He will say about it. The Lord knows that I need a house and He will fix it for me. Now this is my key point in this example of faith at work for you; "the Lord knows our needs" so all we have to do is put our faith to work for us.

I then decided to put my faith into action. Now this may sound crazy to some of you who may not believe, but I walked out of that house and walked around it one time giving thanks to the Lord and counting it done. Then I came to the front door of the house, as I was listening to the owner agree to sell the house to the man from the investment company, I just said thank you Jesus. I then laid my hands upon that house and said Lord you know that I need this house and I count it done, in Jesus name.

Now with me not having enough money to purchase the house and in spite of the owner agreeing to sell the house to the investment company I believed that the Lord would work it out for me. By faith I said to the owner I will wait to hear from you and bided them good-by. My faith was now at work.

Two days later the owner of that house called me and said he was going to sell the house to me. His reply was he would feel better by doing this. My reply was "thank you Jesus." I must tell you that my down payment was now less than he was asking before and the cost of the house was much less than the previous asking price. "What a mighty God we serve." Now this was an example of me putting my faith to work for my need of a house, whatever your needs are, put your faith to work. Victory is on your side. Satan will come at you with all kinds of problems but don't fear. Your faith is bigger than any problem that will come against you.

These are some words that come from one of the many songs my mother would sing:

> Let Jesus fix it for you He Knows just
> What to do, whenever you pray just
> Let Him have His way, let Jesus
> Fix it for you.

So often I think of my mother, She was a wonderful woman of faith and of course she was also a great inspiration in my life. During the time I was growing up as a little boy, my mother would often speak the words of faith into the lives of my brothers, sisters, and myself. Even as little kids she would say to us that the Lord is present with us to hear our prayer. She would tell us to have faith, trust in him, and always believe that He will make a way for you. Prayer was an important part of our family structure. I cherish the memory of our prayer time together as little kids growing coming up, at 8:pm. Each night we would have family prayer. Yes" my mother would teach us to pray and I want you to know that if you just pray and believe all things are possible.

Faith has been instilled into my spirit at an early age. I must say to you that I believe God can do anything but fail. Because of my mother, my faith and trust is rooted in the Lord. As I am writing this book now, it seems like I can hear my mom's voice saying to me at this very moment; "the Lord will fix it for you, just trust Him He will fix it." My mother has since gone to be with the Lord. She made that great transition over twenty-five years ago, but thanks be to God for the memories of such a wonderful woman.

I think for the most part, I had always been an optimistic person. I believe that some times out of adversity come of life very finest moment. I don't give up so quickly in what I believe. I am the kind of person who had always had the feeling that there was at least "one more bounce in the ball." We should not be so quickly to give up on the promises of God. Just because it may seem like it is not going to work out, or your prayers is not being answered "wait." It is not really over until God say it is over.

In this walk of faith we must have the kind of trust that even in the darkest hour of trials in our life we can keep moving forward. As believers, we learn how to rest in Lord and wait patiencely on Him. We must come to the realization that the Lord is not going to fix all of our problems at the very moment they arise. There are some things we must go through. Through the trials of life, I have come to realize that troubles has a substantial amount of ingredients in our lives, it is the character that we develops from it.

The fact remains that at appointed times through the permissive' will of God, He permits trouble in all of our lives. Therefore it is so important for us to patiently wait on the Lord and trust Him, for He, is bringing us to spiritual growth and purpose. He will come through for you just trust Him. The Lord will show up on time. This know also; your trials through patience of faith builds great character in you. There will be many obstacles along the way in this walk of faith. Times will come when Satan, who is the opposite of good will try to interrupt us on our journey, but you have power over the works of Satan. By faith we will keep moving forward knowing that God got our back. He is with us every step of the way. The Lord tells us from His Holy word; "I will never leave you, nor forsake you, I will be with you all ways."

> God is faithful to His word,
> So we must trust him.

Take courage to know that great is the faithfulness of God. He cannot lie. The Lord is committed to us through His love, a love that cannot fail. As we put our trust in Him, in spite of the circumstances we may encounter we have the assurance from the word of God that He never fails. Therefore, through faith as you line up your will with the will of God, those things that you desire of him shall come to pass.

The Lord is pleased in your unwavering trust in him, and faith in none other. He is our God who is there to supply all of our needs. He is there to help in time of trouble. You may be struggling with some financial problems as most of us have at one time or another. I do understand how the concern of it can become a burden to you as you are trying to care for and provide for you family. You must be encouraged and know that there is nothing too hard for God. You can take all of your burdens to the Lord for He cares for you, we have a God who supplies all of our needs. The Lord ears are open unto the cry of his people. Why? It is because He is concerned about our cares. As I so often say, He is an ever-active concerned God; we can call on him by faith at any time.

When I think of the faithfulness of the Lord, I cannot help but think of Him also who is our faithful friend. He is a friend like no other. When every one else has turned their backs on you, the Lord will never leave you. There is a song my mother would sing sometime, it was so comforting to hear her sing it, Joseph M. Scriven is the person who wrote it. Here are some of the words:

> *What a friend we have in Jesus, all our sins and griefs to bear!*
> *What a privilege to carry every-thing to God in prayer!*
> *O what peace we often forfeit, O what needless pain we bear,*
> *All because we do not carry every- thing to God in prayer!*
>
> *Have we trials and temptations? Is there trouble anywhere?*
> *We should never be discouraged; Take it to the Lord in prayer.*
> *Can we find a friend so faithful who will all our sorrows share?*

Jesus knows our every weakness; Take it to the Lord in prayer.

God is faithful to His word but we must trust Him. As we read in Psalms 23: 4a. King David speaks of his contentment in the Lord "Yea though I walk through the valley of the shadow of death, I will fear no evil: for thou art with me." Comforting faith is our complete dependence on the Lord for provision, guidance, and protection.

When you really think about it, it is so comforting to know that the Lord is with us always. God is with us when times are going well in our lives and when He permits the trying times to come in our life to test our faith. By faith, we should always be able to sense the presence of the Lord with us even in times of trouble. Another good point to know is this; the Lord will not allow us to suffer more than we can bear (1 Cor.10: 13.) God have given us the faith to keep moving forward, we just have to use it.

The danger in not using your faith to trust God is that you grant Satan the liberty to influence a deceiving spirit of unbelief into your mind. Unbelief is your lack of faith, or distrust in God. When we fail to trust God, the power of Satan is greater to work through us and against us of sickness, trouble, disease, anger, and other influences of evil works. Therefore our faith is the weapon or instrument of war against Satan evil works, your faith is mighty through God to the pulling down of strong holds, and bring onto captivity every thought to the obedience of Christ.

The point that I try to make very clear in this book is based on two words "absolute or positive faith." my reason for using these words as much as I do is of their importance. The two words are one in the same, in their certain of belief as it relates our to faith. Its importance is the assured faith we have in the Lord. It gives us the drive to stay focused in our belief and trust in God. This kind of faith gives us the determination to stand against all odds in our wait: our absolute faith displays our confidence in the Lord. It sends a notice to Satan of our positive stand: "I shall not be move."

One other quality I need to point out here on absolute or positive faith, which it is our openly expressed affirmation in the power of God. Even when every one else has given up, you will be found still standing with conviction that some how, some way God will come through. The Lord will show up on time. God never fails, your best friend may walk away from you, and yes, regretfully to say even family members may turn their backs on you, but be assured the Lord never fails.

As a Christians we will never know our spiritual strength in faith and what we can do until we have experienced the pressure of the battle. Our faith will be tested through trials and temptations to see if we really do believe what we say as we affirm our unwavering faith in God.

Chapter 4

Life After the Fall

We can be assured of one inescapable fact of life: we will certainly experience interruptions in our lives at one time or another. These interruptions are the various trials, troubles and hindrances that we are confronted with on a daily basis, much of which is unavoidable. At some point in this life we are going to come upon hard bumps along the road. There will be many times that life will throw some fast curve balls at us. No matter how skillful we may be in avoiding most of them, some balls will hit us because we just could not dodge them. To imagine that no troubles will befall us is like wishing not to live at all; troubles are a necessary part of this transient world.

We are going to experience twists and turns and rise and falls in life. These are inescapable. Each of us is going to encounter various trials in life, and with these troubles comes the pain. However, our reaction to this will determine the effects of the outcome. As a little boy growing up, I would always hear these words of wisdom from my grandfather to those who were experiencing troubles in their lives: "The wiles of life will introduce itself to each of us at various times in our life, but the way in which we react to it will determine the kind of foundation we are building for ourselves." You see, no matter how peculiar we are in trying to do our best in life, we are going to have some pitfalls along the way. But the difference is in how we respond and confront the challenges we encounter.

Challenges will come and create disturbances in our life. But we must be careful not to be deceived by the works of Satan; this will enable us to respond to our troubles in a positive way. What I am saying here is we must not allow the devil to slip in unaware and cause us to lose hope and fall into a state of discouragement. If this happens, it is probably because we were not paying attention to his tricks. His job is to entice us to do wrong and, if we are not careful in our moment of weakness, we will submit to his tricks and fall into the temptations of his deception. It is also necessary for me to say to you that in this life we are not free from any of the ills of trouble, disappointment, sickness, disease, hurt, pain, or loss. It is just the opposite; these interruptions are the very essence of life. These interruptions can become our biggest fears because of our wavering mind; these hindrances occur so frequently in life that at times we feel like there is no end to our troubles.

A common mistake most people make in life is allowing fear from sorrows and trouble to entice them to quit; usually this appears to be the first available alternative. The temptations to give up, quit and fall by the wayside, to do wrong or commit some ungodly act knock at all doors, and a majority of the troubled will answer the enticing call. Fear will tell you that there is no way out of your troubles, no help in view, and you should just give up and quit. The question to ask is: What will cause you to surrender to your fears? We surrender when we allow ourselves to be deceived by the temptation of Satan himself. He tries to influence you to think that quitting is an easier way out of your troubles than to wait on your deliverance through faith, as you fight the good fight of faith. Through his enticement if you allow him to, he will bring you to the conclusion that all hope is gone. If you give in to the fear created by his evil influences, he will trouble your mind with doubt causing you to believe that no one cares and you are all alone or no one understands you.

Then there are those daily frustrations in life that can slowly wear you down little by little by just pecking away at your joy, pecking away at your peace, and your patience and strength. These daily frustrations sometimes take such a toll on us that we feel we no longer have a leg to stand on. When this happens, we become emotionally detached and vulnerable. We fall out of marriage, out of family, out of our job, out of the love for God, and even out of life itself. The stress that is caused by the over concerns of the pressures of life can result in health problems. It can also cause problems in our thoughts, in feelings, in our actions and in our spiritual life, which will negatively impact our relationship with God. There are three approaches to coping with stress and the frustrations of life that can cause people to fall.

First, people **deny** or imagine the problem doesn't really exist. Second, people **avoid** or run away from the problem hoping it will fix itself. Third, they become detached. They allow themselves to become so overwhelmed with the stresses of life that they **withdraw**, give up and turn in the wrong direction in life. When we fail to respond to the pains of life in a positive way, the outcome of the situation is more likely to be unbeneficial. We must confront and respond to our problems and challenges of life with positive faith expecting good results.

Life is full of troubles, and it also has a way of giving us what we expect from it. It's called the self-fulfilling prophecy. There are so many people who seem to always anticipate the worst out of their troubles. People who are always anticipating negative results in time of trouble are more likely to experience just that. In Job's dialogue with his friends (Job 3:25) he said, "For the things which I greatly feared is come upon me, and that which I was afraid of is come unto me." There is an old adage that says if you go through life always expecting bad things to happen, life will oblige.

Then there are disappointments, which can deprive you of your courage and confidence. But if we would each day deliberately practice giving God thanks and praising Him for who He is and whose we are, we will be blessed with renewed strength and courage. He will activate new sources of strength, energy and power within us to keep moving forward even after we have fallen. In spite of our circumstances, there is hope we can live life anew. What we must understand is that every apparent setback is only temporary and in the reality of our faith, it is only a setup for a greater tomorrow.

Fear which arises from the stress of emotional interruptions and circumstances in life challenges our faith and torments our minds. It deceives us into believing that there is no hope for us, and that we should just give in to the fear. Fear leads to doubt, and then doubt will produce uncertainty and disbelief. Uncertainty and disbelief causes us to give in to the temptation of quitting. It will lead us to the conclusion that there is no need to try any longer because we fail to see a reason to go on. When we give in to the temptation of fear and doubt, it will lead us into making bad choices and wrong decisions in life. The problem in allowing ourselves to be so overwhelmed with emotional fear and uncertainty is the possibility of becoming predisposed to unwise and destructive actions and spiritual ruin.

A great number of people, who struggle with various troubles in life as well as failures, harbor these emotional scares and become immersed in their fears. They find themselves in a troubled frame of mind, they feel isolated and begin to withdraw as they gradually become mentally engulfed in deep depression. Anyone who is so overpowered by their grief from life's ills and is living in fear and disbelief is at a very tenuous state in their life. Failure to seek help can possibly lead to an even more serious threat to their mental state of mind. Such mental condition causes destructive behaviors, and if appropriate help is not sought for these perplexities, their behavior could also lead to spiritual or physical suicide.

Regardless of how careful we are, the trials of life may come upon us without warning. If we lose hope in time of trouble when we really need to be courageous, we will fall out of the race of life due to the fears of our expectation. God gives us purpose in life. Therefore, we shouldn't fall by the wayside and become submerged in fear and uncertainty, instead we must hold on to faith, hope and aspiration which will move us forward toward our destiny. We must be unyielding and refuse to wallow in self pity. Our recourse must be our determination to get up, brush ourselves off, and get back in the race with our eyes on the prize. We have to always be willing to start all over again in life when we need to do so. When those times come, and they will, we have to muster up all our strength to move forward. The Lord did not put us here on this earth to be losers or quitters. As a little boy, my dad would often tell me that one who cannot survive bad times will not see good times. Then he would say "son, a tree can't be felled with one stroke."

Do you know that in the Lord we are more than conquerors? It does not matter whether you are rich or poor, through faith we all can be winners in the trials of life. Therefore, it is so important for us to learn how to react positively in a negative situation. If anyone is in need of wisdom, let him ask of God, but he must ask in faith not wavering (doubting). So put your faith to work for your success in life.

Without faith you will not be able to recognize the answer the Lord is sending you concerning deliverance in your situation. For this reason, you must ask in faith as you believeth in Him. As believers, we are encouraged to have unwavering faith, which keeps us connected to the promises of God as we are confronted by and respond to the challenges of life. If you have fallen by the wayside, my friend, you may still be experiencing the after effects of your defeat in one way or another, even as you are trying to make a new start in life. But you must be determined to bounce back with the goal to overcome past failures. You will experience down days and moments of discouragement; yet you must resist the temptation to give up and fall back into the spirit of defeat. Through faith, you will find yourself bouncing back with a new enthusiasm for life. If you are steadfast in your quest for good outcomes in the challenges you encounter, there is life and greater life after these interruptions.

Here is another point of importance I need to make: to avoid a defeated spirit. You should never be so overwhelmed in your circumstances that you are unable to function mentally or physically. The overload of a defeated spirit is negative weight, which hinders you from moving forward in a more positive manner. As a young adult trying to establish my independence many years ago, I recalled a statement my mother made. Even to this day, her words of encouragement have been a source of strength to me during low times in my life. These were her words: "Failure is a juncture in the road; it must never become a campground." And she continued: "So we pack up our tents and move on to greener pastures." We must have this kind of faith and determination to keep moving forward in spite of the interruptions that are sure to come our way. Do you not know that people who have strong faith in God are never ultimately defeated? The reason is because they just simply refuse to accept failure of any kind.

A friend of mine who is the pastor of a large congregation in Jackson, Ms. has achieved respectable success as a pastor. He stated to me, "Failures are the pillars to success." My friend endured much defeat in the past before he arrived at this favorable outcome in his ministry. He learned how to use his defeat as stepping-stones to become the successful pastor he is now. Faith will give us the assurance that we can turn our scars into stars; we can be better because of our brokenness; we are not alone, no we are never alone. We are more than conquerors through Him that loved us (Rom.8: 37).

So you have fallen, what now? Is this the time to give up and quit, to relinquish your goals in life? Should you stop because it seems like no one cares or is willing to lend a helping hand? These questions are asked in the book of Jeremiah 8:4: "Shall they fall, and not arise? Shall He turn away, and not return"? Be encouraged, you can get back up again to be better than you were before. Don't let anyone tell you that you can't; you must tell yourself you can. Learn how to encourage your own self. Get up and get back into the race; wanting more out of life is the incentive to go forward. Satan will place uninvited and unwelcome thoughts in your mind to give up and quit, but you must turn those negative thoughts into positive thoughts in order to move forward: I will succeed in life, I am not a failure, I will not give up, and I can do all things through Christ who strengthens me!!!

Even though you may have made some bad decisions in your life and taken some wrong turns of which you are ashamed, you don't have to live in defeat. There may be things in your past or even in the present you are ashamed to face, that are very painful, but you don't have to be ashamed. It is always better to confront those issues you are concealing so that you may be able to move forward. You must make peace with yourself and then with others, and not submerge your thoughts on past failures. There are so many people who allow the shame and guilt of their past to enslave them. That is why it is important that we confront our issues so we may move forward. Do not let past failures to deter you from your destiny neither should you allow them to define your future.

We have to let go of the anger, hostility and bitterness that keep us separated and unable to be in fellowship with others. We all have a desire to love and be loved, but in order to have healthy relationships, it is essential that we make peace with ourselves and with others. In order for you to move forward with your life, it may be necessary, if possible and under the right circumstances, for you to go and ask for forgiveness of those you have wronged.

The mistakes and wrong turns you have made in life may have you now feeling uncertain about your future, but you must put that in your past and move forward. We learn from our mistakes, hurts and failures; we grow and become wiser and move on. We don't dwell on the hurts or mistakes of our past; it may be necessary for us to regroup and start over again with a new outlook on life. It may be necessary after a fall to transplant ourselves. There are many people today who are esteemed to new life only after transplanting themselves. The statue on the altar will never be venerated by someone who saw it when it was part of a tree trunk in the forest.

In spite of how people may view you now or based on your past, be encouraged to know that the God who loves us all is a God of second chances. In 1 John 1:1 it is written: "If any man sin, Jesus Christ the righteous is our advocate:" He defends us, He brings blessings upon us, and it is He who restores us back to the father. Know this also, you are not the only one who has made mistakes in life, and please believe me neither will you be the last. I can understand how it feels when people look down on you as if they have never made a mistake in life or done any wrong. I am well acquainted with those who are so self-righteous that they think they are the only ones walking with Jesus. There is a Jewish quotation that says: "A faultless man is possible only in a faultless world." The Bible tells us in Romans 3:23, "For we all have sinned, and come (fall) short of the Glory of God."

We all need to ask the Lord for forgiveness of our sins. Furthermore, God's grace is there for those who have fallen from grace. You could be one of those who have fallen because of the hurt and shame you may have suffered from a co-laborer in ministry. Hurt that comes from within can be very discouraging because if anyone should know how to esteem their brothers and sisters to good works, it should be our co-laborers in the house of the Lord. If anyone should know how to forgive, to keep the peace, and to love as Christ teaches us to love, it should be our Christian brothers and sisters. You see, there are those who want to appear to be faultless and feel they are justified in condemning their brother. They fail to realize that they also need God's mercy.

The Bible tells us that love covereth all sins. In other words, we shouldn't hold on forever to a mistake made by our brother or sister that they may have committed in the past. We should have enough love of Christ in us to restore them who may have fallen, in the same way as we would like to be restored if we ourselves had fallen. Therefore, we should be willing and ready at all times to forgive and receive our brother and sister back into the fold. It is because of failure to live by this principle of forgiving others that we have run multitudes of people away from the house of the Lord. When we hold ourselves up as better than they are, we are saying that we are above reproach and never make the mistakes that others make in life. How dwells the love of God in you?

BE DETERMINED TO MAKE IT IN SPITE

OF YOUR CIRCUMSTANCES

I wholeheartedly agree, my fallen brothers and sisters, that disappointments can be discouraging, they can be a great let down, and may even cause you to become emotionally detached. Because of the hurt, you may find yourself giving in to the temptation to quit in life. But you don't have to wallow in your hurt even if no one seems to care enough to pick you up. Don't give up and lose your self-esteem, you can encourage yourself. Get yourself up and get back in the race.

You are not defeated!! That is a lie the devil is trying to put in your spirit. He will say that all have turned their backs on you and that you are a failure. The devil will go as far as to tell you that there is no need to go any further, that you should quit and give up, because no one really cares. Satan is a deceiver; he doesn't want you to know that you can make it in spite of past failures. Someone once told me, "Failures are the pillars to success." It is not the will of the Lord that you should give up. We have the opportunity now to be stronger, wiser, better than ever before. Let us not allow the works of Satan to stop us from doing whatever is needed for all those who cross our path. The door is open; move on to greatness. The Lord is there to help you.

As I am writing this chapter, "Life after the fall," I am reminded of a time in my life when I was extremely discouraged. I was at the point of almost giving up because I felt hopeless and defeated. This interruption was caused by my co-laborers in ministry, to be specific pastors, men of my equal. They deliberately and viciously attacked my ministry that God had so faithfully blessed me with; their strategy was to destroy my ministry and character with the hope that I would give up and turn away from God. You see, there are some people who say they love the Lord, but are unrepentant and will allow the Devil to set up evil in their hearts against you. This unrepentant attitude displayed by these brethren emanated from a spirit of jealousy.

My co-laborers in ministry caused me as well as others to suffer much hurt and loss of fellowship, all because of their wrong doings motivated by jealousy. The Bible tells us in Song of Solomon 8:6b that "jealousy is cruel as the grave." These brethren allowed evil to motivate them. They were envious of how well the Lord had blessed my ministry in the short time I had been in the area.

They had been pasturing for many years, but their ministries were not going as well as they would have liked. My church membership was growing much faster than expected and we were preparing to do even greater kingdom works for the Lord. So mischief and deceit began to set up in their hearts. Their failure to produce growth in their ministry moved them to be angry at the way in which God was blessing the work of my ministry. So their plot was to tear down the success bestowed by the Lord on my ministry.

As previously stated, the wrong that was inflicted by these three brethren brought me to a devastating low, to the point of almost giving up. This was a spiritually painful process for me and others, and a learning experience as well. In circumstances such as this, the temptation is ever present to give up, fall out of grace and be resentful, but I refused to allow Satan to have victory in this situation. There will come times in your life when you will have to be determined not to allow yourself to give up and fall by the way-side but have a positive attitude towards your outcome. As stated before, wanting more out of life should be your incentive to go forward.

The tests and trials that I had suffered was a great struggle to endure; my daily prayer was that the Lord would help me to maintain a forgiving spirit, and not be resentful. It would be erroneous for me to say to you that I was not angry. Was I angry? Absolutely! Of course I was, very much so. The deception and calculated attacks on my ministry and my character by my brethren of the cloth was not only wrong, but also evil. They allowed their jealous spirit to control their actions and way of thinking. But God brought me through it. I am so thankful because my faith in God is so deeply rooted I was able to endure and rise above it all.

I cannot begin to imagine the devastating effects and consequences of a situation such as this on someone who is not strong in faith. This type of deliberate negative action against someone could result in severe discouragement and profound disappointment. Someone who is weak in spirit can lose hope and fall out of grace in a situation such as this, with no hope of ever recovering from it.

So we should be very careful in how we treat people and consider their feelings. We should treat people the way we would like to be treated. Sometimes hurt from within can be very devastating to your spirit. When I was going through my difficult situation I was determined not to let Satan gain victory from my test. There were times I had to encourage myself and speak overcoming faith into my spirit. I would reassure myself that I was going to bounce back from this terrible circumstance because God was going to see me through it. You must know within yourself that if God brings you to it, He will see you through it. When there seems to be no one to encourage you, you must encourage yourself. Speak victory over the challenges you are facing and into your spirit and the results of your outcome will be good.

Those of you who have fallen, you must now learn from it. If it was failure on your part, be sure that you learn well because the old adage is: experience is the best teacher. Beloved, you must learn how to encourage yourself, be courageous in your quest to overcome, and have a positive attitude praying always. And don't ever allow your troubles to deter you from praying! God will put people in your life that will support you and will pray with you in your time of trouble. He did just that for me.

I thank God for bringing me through my situation with victory. The suffering, pain, embarrassment and loss that I endured were bearable because the Lord lifted me through it all, and He can do the same for you if you trust Him. While I was going through my pain, I did not hold any resentment or seek revenge against my co-laborers. I was damaged, but God delivered me. I was able to bounce back in victory and become much stronger spiritually because of my determination to stay in the grace of God.

The good news is God did not allow this wrong to go unresolved. I was able to forgive them for the wrong that was done to me, and these brethren and I have reconciled. As I reflect on this trying experience of twenty years ago, I can safely say that I did my utmost not to fail God. Since then, two of these brethren have passed on and I learned that one other brother is still pasturing a small congregation, but has suffered much hurt, shame, and embarrassment due to some wrongdoing and ungodly choices he has made in his life. My prayers are that the Lord will help him and all those who have gone astray, that they will find peace and wholeheartedly return to the grace of God.

LOVE YOURELF

In the Bible, the question is asked: "Why sit we here until we die?" Get yourself up! Live your life to the fullest; there is so much to be done in your family life, your community, and church. Where is your confidence? The man who has confidence in himself gains the confidence of others. You are very special in the eyes of God, we belong to God, and we are of God, the essence of Him. Learn to love yourself and your physical being, give God thanks every day for your body. Do you not know that your body is His most wonderful creation?

We should give God thanks for our body and for the effectiveness of its operation, "for in Him we live, we move and we have our being." We should make it a practice each day to give God thanks for this wonderful creation, from our head down to our toes. Thanksgiving will produce joy and satisfaction. Our body is the temple of our soul; therefore, we should glorify the Lord in our body and soul. We are God's workmanship. When we live a life of gratitude and thanksgiving, our lives will be full of joy.

So don't give up, get up! Start to live life anew, it is available now. You can bounce back with new enthusiasm, a new and more positive attitude to do better than before. Each morning after you have risen from bed, and have given thanks to God for a new day and a new beginning, look at yourself in the mirror, and say with great enthusiasm: "I am blessed, and highly favored of the Lord." Do you know that the Lord has favored you for this day to do something good? To blossom as the flower blooms from its bud exhibiting its freshness and glowing beauty?

There is a Chinese proverb that says: tomorrow's plants are in the seeds of today. We cannot recapture yesterday and our past is behind us. We have an opportunity today to start planting our seeds of life. Past failures are just that, past failures. The mistakes we made in the past are now to be learned from, to be stepping-stones to greatness, pillars of success. Tomorrow's plants are in the seeds of today. Have you begun to start planting your seeds of life?

GET STARTED

What a great blessing to have the opportunity to start over again! You can have a fresh new start and a new beginning from defeat. Getting a handle on spiritual growth is crucial; it is God's will and command for all, not an option. If we want to please God, we should make the best of our new start. You may not be able to leap over high mountains or climb the tall skyscrapers of life at this time, but you can start by putting Christ first in your life and developing a positive attitude toward spiritual growth.

We must understand that a negative attitude will hold us back from growth. As I have stated: spiritual growth is crucial. Our circumstances will never change for the better if we continue to allow our negative attitude to hold us back from growing spiritually; it will only continue to produce destructive unwanted results. The probability that someone with a negative attitude will achieve positive results is slim to none. Conversely, someone with a positive attitude is more likely to experience positive outcomes.

If we are serious about a new start in life and growing spiritually, we must pursue a loving relationship with Christ, which will deepen as we get to know Him better. Spiritual growth demands nourishment, as stated in 1 Pet. 2:2 "like newborn babies, long for the pure milk of the Word, so that by it you may grow in respect to salvation." Spiritual growth has its purpose; it is also a process of developing good character. As I have stated, in this life we are going to encounter trials, they are indispensable to our spiritual growth. Growth is God's will for us. The alternative to growth is stagnation and eventual deformity. What we must understand is that failing to grow is not an option for a believer, that is, if you really want to please God.

It could be that you are facing an uphill battle as you get started in your new spiritual walk. It will take time to build strong faith and trust in Christ, but you can start by focusing on Christ and His Glory. Make positive statements about your situation. Absolutely avoid saying: "I am not going to make it through this, or this is so awful, there is no hope, there is no way this can work out for my good, or it's hopeless." Again, a negative outlook emphasizes failure; a positive outlook reflects success.

The decisions that we make in advance concerning our circumstances, be it good or bad, will have an effect on the results of the outcome. You can decide yourself into a mental mess or into mental peace, into good results or bad results, into happiness or unhappiness. Your decision will impact your outcome. You can rise up from failure and move positively toward your desirable outcome. Keep in mind that by having a negative attitude toward your new start in life, the results of it will be in line with your expectation.

I have found that when you put Christ first in your life, you will have the ammunition to face the hard realities of life with confidence. Knowing that God is there to help you through trying times, you are able to resolve tough situations and come out unscathed. There is always the possibility of things going bad in your life, but with a good positive attitude and the Lord at your side, you can change the situation around you for the better. So yes, there is life after a fall, by putting God first, and being determined to succeed in life in spite of your trying circumstances. So get up from your hurt, your pain, embarrassments, or whatever life ills you may be suffering from. Even if you have made some bad choices and wrong decisions, you do not have to be a victim of your circumstances. You can bounce back stronger and wiser, turning your failures into pillars of success. What is so refreshing for us to know is that as we acknowledge the Lord, He will direct our paths. So go for it!

Words of wisdom
To live by

Always behave as though others are watching. A man who looks after his actions knows that others see him, or will. He knows that walls have ears, and that what is badly done is bursting to become known. Even when he is alone, he behaves as though the entire world is watching, and knows that all will be revealed. He behaves as though he already had witnesses: those who, when they hear something, will be so later.

Here are some final words of encouragement. Remember: Time is not elastic. It cannot be stretched or manipulated. You owe it to yourself to do all you can to get the most out of it right now! Don't let the anxiety of fears from past failures keep you from having the kind of life you desire. If you allow yourself to be inhibited by the anxiety of fears from past failures, hurts and emotional scars, you will not get what you want out of life. To move forward, you should develop a positive attitude believing in Christ that all things are possible. Tell yourself that things will get better and with Christ you can succeed. Integrate this self-help strategy into your daily life and discover in yourself the confident, fulfilled, productive person you desire to be.

We have an ever-active God who is always concerned about our every need. So the opportunity is now for you to go on with your life, and be better than before, and you will achieve! The Word of God provides this assurance, "I can do all things through Christ that strengtheneth me" (Phil.4:13). Through

Elder G. E. Johnson

Christ, you are capable of succeeding and you must not allow distractions to take your eyes off your destination. Don't let your past dictate your future. Forge ahead with Christ and live the life he has planned for you.

CHAPTER 5

The Torment of Suffering: You Don't Have to Give Up

As I begin this chapter on the torment of suffering, allow me to offer some significant reasons for our suffering. First of all, there are times our suffering can come from God because it is essential to our spiritual growth, as it develops an eternal perspective toward purpose. Then, there are other times in our life the suffering that we endure serves to develop within us a willing attitude for Christ; it also identifies us with other believers. It is necessary for you to know that how you react to the trials of life reflects your beliefs; positive suffering destroys counterfeit faith. Our trials of life also drive us back to the basics of our faith, and we can take heart and rejoice now because one day all of our suffering will end.

Our suffering comes from troubles that vary in degree; they range from mild irritations to full-blown catastrophes. Because our personalities are different, our responses to trouble also vary, but the way in which we cope and respond to trouble will have a great effect on the results of the outcome. And know this, troubles are not limited to a select few; man is born into trouble as the sparks fly upward. Job, 5:7.

Trouble doesn't discriminate nor are we exempt from it. No one is excluded from some form of suffering because everyone experiences trouble. Sometimes, it comes with advance warning. We watch the storm clouds develop, but cannot turn them back.

At other times, there is no warning: seemingly out of a cloudless sky, tragedy strikes. We struggle beneath its battering winds and we cry out, "Where is God?" Sometimes, like Job, we wonder if we have believed in vain. But Job says (Job 14: 14b.) "All the days of my appointed time will I wait, till my change come." Cor. 10:13 tells us that God is faithful, who will not suffer you to be tempted above that you are able. It is so encouraging to know and is very clear that God also provides strength in time of crisis. Isaiah 40: 29-31 reminds us: "Therefore we should not be so quick to give up on hope, because even in the mist of calamity there is opportunity.

It must also be stated that there are times we bring trouble upon ourselves. Sometimes, the consequence of our suffering comes from bad and irresponsible decisions and actions that we cause upon ourselves. The trouble and calamity that we bring upon ourselves call for our willingness to repent and confess any and all known wrongs we have committed. But to assume that every trouble or tragedy that comes into our lives is a direct result of personal sin is to join Job's three friends in their cruel assessment of Job's dilemma (Job 4:1-2, 7-9. 8: 1-8. 11: 17).

There are those moments when we suffer from the very wrong that others inflict upon us. Sometimes, our suffering is a direct attack by Satan on our lives. Then, there are the times when our suffering comes to shape us for special service. And there are the times we don't know why we are suffering. It is at this point that we must be willing to trust God in spite of unanswered questions. Here is a quotation from my mother: "If you want to live in this world, equip yourself with a heart that can endure suffering."

From my personal experience, I can safely say to you that there will be particular periods in our lives when the torment of suffering can be extremely and unpleasant for us to bear. Trials such as this can be like no other you have ever experienced before, but even in these kinds of trials we should be encouraged to know that we have control over the outcome. We must always bear in mind that the same God who brought us through all of the other tribulations in the past, as painful as the present trials may be He is the One who will carry us through this with joy. Nothing is impossible with God.

As we encounter the various trials in our life, there are times the reality of suffering may cause us to question ourselves: "Where did I go wrong?" "What could I have done differently?" My answer to you is this: we can try to do all the right things, but we still have to come to the understanding that our trials are essential to our spiritual growth; trials are unavoidable.

Normally, trials and suffering come unscheduled and are usually unwelcome. They always seem to come at the worst possible times. Although trials and suffering are not easy to deal with, they are painful, hurtful and can be very embarrassing, but we do have control over the outcome. God will not put any more on us than we can handle so we have control over the element of our trials and suffering. It is in the way we look at our suffering and trials of faith and how we respond to it.

The reality of suffering is the state of enduring physical or mental pain. Distress, loss or injury endured, it is the toleration of pain and punishment. The torment of suffering is the torture and anguish it causes. Suffering seems to drain all of the strength out of you. Your faith through patience will play a major role in the renewal of your strength if you wait in hope. But, in this world of instant gratification which may cause us to lose the ability to wait on the lord, we expect to learn patience in a hurry. You see, we need to know the Lord through the fellowship of His suffering, but at that moment we tend to ask for instant results. Relief from pain is at the top of our list, but patience comes from experience, and experience gives us hope.

Sometimes, our suffering can be very hurtful, painful, and embarrassing and this can bring us to a point of giving up. The hurt, pain, and embarrassment from suffering can be a tremendous load for us to bear; it can reduce our strength to a new low in our life. It can weigh so heavily on us that it becomes difficult to pray; we just can't seem to find the words to say. It seems like the Lord is so far away, and we are just too low to reach Him. "When the heart is full, the eyes overflow." Dear hearts, I must tell you, I've been at that point, the point of almost giving up. "But the devil is a liar." You don't have to give up! You can't give up! And you can make it if you do not lose hope. Although the effects that follow from the trials of your suffering are very hard to bear, we must resolve within ourselves to stand firm in our belief when life's ills are trying to make us bitter and hopeless.

In times of trouble, every individual must learn to speak the word of faith over the circumstances that they are experiencing. You must speak the words of faith for renewed strength and deliverance looking forward to a favorable outcome. I am able to joyfully tell you from many personal victories, when the devil thought he really had brought me to defeat, the Lord brought me out with victory. As I am speaking to you through the writing of this book, I must inform you the Lord is right there, right now, where you are. You can reach Him now; He is there to deliver you. Through your faith and patience, He will renew your strength. Trust and Wait on the Lord; wait, I say, on the Lord; victory shall be yours.

I must also inform you that, as Christians, our trials are not purposeless. We will come to realize as believers in Christ that our trials and tests of faith perfect us. They also are indispensable to our spiritual growth. You see, we cannot grow as we should without trials; though we may suffer much, our trials better us. Our suffering and trials in this life are designed with us in mind; they are custom-made with our names on them. God designs our trials with purpose; as painful as they may be, they are designed to fit our spiritual needs and launch us to our next spiritual level of faith.

As we endure the trials in this life, it is from the Word of God that we will draw the strength and encouragement we need to keep moving forward. Just because you may be suffering some hardship in your life at this very moment, there is no need to turn back or give up. We are encouraged through the Word of the Lord in Psa.34: 15, 19: "The eyes of the Lord is upon the righteous, and his ears are upon their cry. Many are the afflictions of the righteous; but the Lord delivereth him out of them all."

These afflictions and trials sometimes come as an adverse set of circumstances in our lives. They are either permitted by God or created by Him for our spiritual growth and development. Although they can be painful and costly to us, the one thing we can be assured of is this: God is in control. Our trials serve a good purpose although we may not recognize this when we are suffering through them, but in the end we grow and mature spiritually. Knowing this as well, our trials and tests of faith produce endurance, as we let it perfect and make us complete in Him; we will then lack in nothing. Please read Jas. 1:3-4. As we faithfully endure our trials, they refine us so that Jesus Christ may be reflected in our lives.

There are seasons in our life when, through the permissive will of God, our suffering has to take its course. In other words,

Elder G. E. Johnson

you are going to have to go through some things sometime. I have come to realize as a believer that there will be times when God will send us our trials directly or he will allow them to come. They are all by the will of God and for His purpose. Now please know there is no problem that God can't bring you through; no problem he can't fix regardless of the circumstances you may be experiencing. While you endure the hardship and the hurt of pain, know that the Lord will give you peace. Yes, He will give peace to endure the realities of life. You can have peace in the midst of your suffering. And, while you wait, the Lord will also strengthen you. Peace gives you a state of rest or calmness from the disturbance of suffering.

Suffering sometimes causes
Embarrassment.

An essential point that should be realized in this chapter is the importance of giving God praise. We, as believers, can praise God for victory in advance. As believers, we have control over the results of our trials, so we don't have to quit thereby giving Satan the victory. The Lord will not bring you to it if He could not carry you through it. Our trials are to bring us to spiritual maturity. There may come times when God will allow your suffering to be put on public display. Many of us have had moments as this in life. We should use the opportunity to our advantage to give God the glory that He may be glorified in you. For it is your time to shine knowing that you are coming out of this situation with victory. The reason we have to encounter trials, as Christians, is that they come with a purpose no matter how severe or painful. As previously stated, they are designed to take us from one level of faith to the next.

The devil, who is a deceiver, will try to mislead you into thinking that you are all alone in the disturbance you may be experiencing. But be assured of this: you are not in this by yourself—God is in control. He is help in time of trouble. He is very present in time of trouble. Fix yourself up each day to be ready for your spiritual battle. Your appearance is on display as well; let your confidence shine. So many people make the mistake of going into their spiritual battle with the appearance as though they have no hope. Encourage yourself every day speaking victory over your suffering anticipating a victorious outcome. What a joy to know that you can change the circumstances in your life by unmovable faith and trust in the Lord.

In writing this necessary chapter in my book, my mind goes back to when I was a little boy growing up with my family. I remember back then we were well blessed due to the hard work of my mother and father. We lived a good decent life; my parents owned rental houses that they would rent to the public, sometimes for free to help families in need. My father who worked for a furniture company was also the owner of his own business that my mother did not participate in due to her faith in God. We had two cars and a truck; yes, life was good. My mother would take us to church every Sunday morning, Sunday night, and sometimes during the week. My mother brought us up in holiness (my brothers, sisters and myself) while my dad would attend another church where the rules were not so strict.

I learned how to trust in the Lord because of the faith and dedication of my mother—she was a remarkable woman. She encountered many disappointments in her life, but she had the kind of faith that some how, some way, the Lord will work things out for her. My mother's testimony was if I just hold out and wait a little while longer, every thing would be all right because the Lord would fix it. But, as life would have it, my dad started making many bad choices and committing wrong actions, including gambling and drinking. Many nights he came home drunk and other nights he would not come home at all.

Even though his behavior was unacceptable, I don't want anyone to think I disrespected my father. That was not the case at all; I loved my father very much. He was good to his children and did teach us many good principles in life to live by. But the bad choices my dad made had a negative impact on our family life. Later in life it caused us to lose everything that they had worked so hard for. The bad decisions and other wrong turns my father took during that time also resulted in my parents' separation.

During the time my mother and father had separated, I was in my early teens. When my father departed, my mother had to bring up the children alone. We suffered much from the hurt, shame and embarrassment; my mom for the first time had to stand in a welfare line to get aid for her children. People don't look at you in the same manner anymore, nor do they respect you as they once did in the past, now that you are in need and suffering hardship. Friends become few. Even as little kids, the pain of loss can be very hurtful and hard to deal with. Life can be very difficult and perplexing, and for a woman trying to provide and care all alone for five children, it was not an easy job to do.

Suffering and trials can make you feel helpless at times, but through faith, as I have always said, "We have control over our outcome; it is in how we respond to our tests." Now when others would have given up and yielded to the temptations of life, my mother remained in the church working faithfully and trusting in the Lord. She was a courageous woman, so often in her care and provision for the necessary needs of her children the demand was far more than the resources. But her courage was evidents of the reserve of her spiritual and moral strength on which she would draw on in time of crisis. Faith and complete trust in God helped my mother to always make the best out of a bad situation; through faith, she could always turn a bad situation into a good solution.

We had moved into a rental house and my mother was able to furnish every room of that house except one room. She would pray day and night in that empty room asking the Lord for help in providing for her children, and to give her strength so that she would not give up on Him. As she was waiting on the Lord, she gave Him praise in advance anticipating a good outcome of her circumstance. With the help and guidance of the Lord, He put it in my mother's heart to utilize that empty room as a dining room to sell lunch and dinners to the public. In listening to and obeying the voice of the Lord, we were well blessed. There was a little shopping center and a saw mill not far from where we lived and people would come five days a week for lunch and dinner. It seemed like they were coming from all over the city. Let me just say, the food business was very good.

> Forgive and be merciful to those
> Who have wronged you.

One of many lessons that my mom would teach my siblings and me was that we must do what is right and do well by all, to forgive them who have wronged us. She was a very good example of the many lessons she would teach us. Mother continued to help those who were in need, including the ones in the past who pointed their finger and made fun of us when we were down and out. My mother had a heart of love; she would even help those who had tried to hurt us just because they could. As previously stated, my mother was a remarkable woman; everyone in the community knew she was willing to put others' needs and their cares before hers. My mother was always thoughtful of others.

More than a year later we learned that my father had taken ill in another city where he lived; he was very sick and there was no one to take care of him. His friends had abandoned him in time of need. As soon as my mother received word of my father's illness, she went to the city where he was living and she brought him back to the city where we lived to care for him. My mother then put my father in the hospital and she cared for him until he passed; my father died of cancer. In this life we will suffer much; you can't escape the reality of life: it has its rough and trying times, good and evil, but God will give you the strength to get through.

As I so often say, I am so thankful for the life and teachings of my mother. Her love and trust in the Lord have taught me so much and today I am better off for it. Because my mother prayed with us when we were young, and taught us the Word of God, I have now come to know the Lord for myself and the wonders of His fellowship. I did not fully understand the testimony my mother gave after she had came out of her trials. However, as I have gotten older and know the Lord for myself, I now understand what she was saying. My mother's testimony was this: "Everything that had happened to me was necessary." And she continued, "It was necessary so that it could bring me to where I am today." As I have stated before, our trials are essential—they are necessary for our spiritual growth.

I have learned from many years of trusting in the Lord that I don't have to give up due to the torment of trials and tests that will come my way. Satan, who is your adversary, is there to obstruct your progress in your walk with God. But be assured that God has given you authority over the works of the devil. Instead of giving up, I have learned how to praise God for what he has already done for me, then I praise Him for the victories He is going to bring into my life. You see, you can praise your way out of trouble and into victory.

Your praise is your joy going into victory. You may be going through some trials at this very moment but don't fear, give God praise. Just tell him: Lord, I thank you and give you praise for who you are, I thank you for every mountain you have brought me over. Thank you, Lord, for every valley you have carried me through, and for the many blessings you have given unto me. If we will just think of what He has already done for us, we cannot help but say, "Thank you, Jesus." We are encouraged to know that if He brought us over the mountain, He will also carry us through the valley. Don't faint; your obstacles will take you higher. The ability is in you to fight and stay in the race to the finish, but you must bring the "will."

All too often as Christians we expect the Lord to immediately intercede in the midst of our crisis and correct whatever is wrong at that very moment. I dare not tell you that the pain from trouble is not real. Whatever suffering you may be enduring at this very moment may feel like it is tearing you down instead of building you up, but it has its purpose. In the Bible (Jas. 1:3-4), He tells us that in purpose of trials we have to take it by faith; we also have a promise from a never failing God.

Although sometimes the weight from the torment of suffering can be tremendously heavy to endure, my suggestion to you is to put your trust in the promises of the Lord. He will see you through. We must also learn to recognize the presence of the Lord. He is with us in the midst of every attack that comes against us. So we do not have to submit to the fear because of the attacks of Satan; he cannot exceed the limits God sets for him. Although you can't control how Satan may attack you, we can always choose how we will respond when it happens. Know that sometimes the greatest trial may not be the pain or loss in our lives; it may be in not being able to understand why God is allowing us to suffer. We must courageously

Elder G. E. Johnson

accept what the Lord allows to happen in our lives and remain faithfully committed to him. The Lord Himself will not allow you to suffer above what you are able to bear.

This we do know: that our trials and sufferings are inescapable; we may encounter them to be physical, financial, relational, or emotional. They may last for days, weeks, or even years. There may be times we may not know the exact reason why we are suffering, but the important thing is how we react in our response to our suffering and willingness to trust God. Remember that our faith produces endurance, and endurance is the ability to hang in there until the trial is over. As people of faith, we don't quit halfway through our test, but we pass our test as we move on to our next level of spiritual maturity.

Through our trials and suffering in life, as believers, we know this very important fact and are encouraged to know that "God is enough." There are times our trials and suffering can be costly, we may lose much. It may be our health, our money, a family member or friend. But when nothing else is left, know that God is enough. He is enough in our lives now and in the future. Our suffering can be very difficult at times, but we must learn to love the Lord regardless of what may come our way. Although we may not always be able to fully understand the pain and suffering that we experience, we must courageously trust God giving Him praise in advance of the outcome. If we just trust him in spite of hurt, the result can lead to a deeper relationship with him and a rediscovering of the Lord as never before.

The fact is this: we have power over the works of Satan who comes to harass us. Knowing this, it should be very inspiring to us. Satan does not have the power (his powers are limited) to have victory over your life. Although he is committed to harassing the people of God, he is also confined or restricted to limited power. God has given you the authority to be victorious over the power and works of the devil. So be encouraged, the way in which we cope with suffering that comes from the troubles in our lives will have a major bearing on the effect the trouble will have on our faith in God. To learn this is really to take a giant stride in spiritual growth and development.

Although trouble may come, be encouraged in your understanding of how very special you are to the Lord. Anyone who is living a saved and holy life before God is living the best life that could ever be lived. Dear hearts, to you who may not be living an acceptable life unto the Lord, I encourage you to get to know Him. Prayers truly from the heart open all the doors in Heaven. Pray and seek after God, who is calling us from darkness into this marvelous light, He will be a father and a friend to you like no other. He will never leave you nor forsake you. The Lord is there to help us in time of trouble. Do you not know that we are a royal priesthood, a holy nation unto God and very precious in his sight? So when the going seems to be rough, look at the jewels you're carrying. It is worth saying again: there is nothing too hard for God.

Chapter 6

As We Forgive Our Debtors

Jesus said in Matt.6: 14, "But if ye forgive not men their trespasses, neither will your Father forgive your trespasses." It is easy for us to ask God for forgiveness, but sometimes we find it very difficult to grant it to others. Whenever we ask God to forgive us for our sins, we should ask ourselves whether we have forgiven the people who have wronged us or forgiven the one who has caused us pain. Have I forgiven him who has refused me? Many years ago when I was a little boy, I remember harboring some resentment and blame with some kids in our community who had stolen my bike. I was very angry. Although they had returned it and asked for forgiveness, it was something I was too angry to do. I also remember a profound statement my mother made back then: "Son, a big part of growing up is learning to forgive." We go through life blaming others for our pain. Blame always brings with it anger and anger is a powerful emotion that can get out of control. It very often causes you to act in an inappropriate way.

When you have suffered wrong from someone and feel terribly hurt, the pain makes it very difficult to forgive, especially when the suffering is caused by those you trusted the most. The wounds from such hurt and pain can be very deep, but in this life we learn to receive blows and to forgive those who insult us. As we forgive, it is the beginning of the healing process. It brings about deliverance and a release to the wounded. I recall the words of an old man (we called him big John) many years ago: "If you take revenge, you will regret it; if you forgive, you will rejoice." To forgive is to grant pardon without harboring resentment.

Unforgiving and unresolved conflicts will not allow you to truly pray for people who have wronged you; you must free yourself of the guilt. The memory of how bad a person may have hurt you in the past can be very hard to let go if you are not willing to forgive them. Forgiveness provides freedom from guilt and enables a person to walk in right relationship with God and man. The things that should be most forgotten are the ones most easily remembered. There is a wonderful quotation by a preacher friend of mine who has been pasturing for many years that relates to forgiveness; it is this: "Not only does memory behave basely, not coming forward when it is needed; it is also foolish, it come to us when it shouldn't." The teaching of Christ imparts these words to us; "But I say unto you, Love your enemies, and pray for them which despitefully use you, and persecute you." Matt. 5: 44. The best remedy for the wrongs others have caused us is to forget them, but sometimes we forget the remedy.

God has given us His Word to live by, His Word is the Holy Bible, and the Bible is the inspired and only infallible Word of God. The Bible is not an option; you can't take out of it what you want and that part of God's Word you don't want to live by, you put it aside. You may find it very hurtful to truly forgive people who have gone out of their way to hurt you or bring you down, but as Christ has forgiven us, we must forgive.

Forgiveness is not an act that is always easily done, but the love of Christ and His example of forgiveness is what brings us to that act of love.

The Bible is not a book that God has given us to live by at our convenience, but it is the whole Word of God that we must live by daily. We may find it to be uncomfortable in some life situations, such as forgive them who have hurt you, or pray for them who don't like you, but we don't take from the Word what is convenient and overlook the rest.

As you may recall in a previous chapter of this book, chapter 4, I spoke of a trial that I had to go through which was very hard for me. It was a test I did not expect and especially whom it came through. These were my co-labors in the gospel, men of my equal. Now, if it was my enemy or one who hated me, I could have borne it. But this mischief and wickedness originated from my brethren of the gospel; their plot and deceit were aimed at hurting my ministry and me.

My ministry at the church where the Lord had blessed me to pastor was doing well; in fact, it was very successful. We were expecting to do even greater works. There were three other pastors in the same jurisdiction as my church whose work was not going as well as they would have liked. They became very jealous of how the Lord was blessing my ministry. As you read chapter 4, you will get a brief insight into how devastating the consequences were for me because of their wickedness and deceitfulness. But I endured, although I suffered much hurt and loss. These pastors of whom I speak were my friends. We had prayed together many times, and always had good fellowship. I had even sent members from my congregation with money to one of them to help his struggling ministry.

When people allow themselves to have a spirit of jealousy and deceit in their heart against you, sometimes it will magnify itself to your hurt in spite of your good deeds. Although, as I stated, I suffered much hurt, loss and even embarrassment, the good news is the Lord was there to help me through it. So I understand the feelings of hurt that can come from people you consider your friends, but I can tell you, if you love God and trust Him you will be able to forgive them who do you wrong. Even though you have been damaged, your faith is on the line. Therefore, don't allow your circumstances to dictate your faith or your spiritual growth--God will bring you through. I have learned from my trials in this life to forgive. It is not going to always be convenient and easy to do. The point I am trying to make here is this: most of the time forgiveness….comes from a heart that has been hurt and broken.

Forgiveness is a precept that Christ concerned Himself with to His last breath. "Forgive them, for they know not what they do." His message of love is central to the Christian ethic. Throughout the Gospels, we encounter again and again Christ's pleas for us to love one another and to forgive our trespassers. But there are times even the most sincere Christians (ministers not excluded) have their angry and ugly episodes, many of them daily or weekly. There are times people of good intent and strong religious persuasion allow themselves to be angry, bitter, spiteful, resentful, and sometimes even hateful. But of all the emotions we experience, lack of love and forgiveness rears its head more than the others. Through Christ, it is possible for us to love our enemies, to return good for evil, and not to bear grudges.

Sometimes the hardest thing for us to do as a Christian is to forgive. The thought of what someone did to you makes it so difficult to forget it, the bad things that person said to viciously damage your character as he did, or the hurt of being deceived by someone in whom you had put your trust. Deception can cause one to fall in a state of depression due to the hurt and disappointment that have been brought upon them by the very wrongful intent of the actor. The pain and hurt that one has encountered is not so easy to forget because your mind is a storehouse.

I have a friend who is a well known Minister and professor at Christian School of Theology (one of the schools of ministry I attended to acquire my Christian education). My friend once said these words to me: "Your mind is a storehouse for the memories and hidden resentments as far back as your childhood." Resentment is the feeling of hurt and anger that damages your emotional existence of survival. But forgiveness of yourself and others who have wronged you can clean up these ill feelings and conflicts you are carrying around inside your head.

As Christians, we are called to forgive. It is a part of our spiritual DNA that connects us with Christ who is our source. We know that we have to forgive in order to have a continuing relationship with the Father. But sometimes the memories can be so sharp and painful, that we just can't forget. What we must realize is that, in forgiving, we lead with the heart. If we forgive "from the heart" then our head will come in line. It is within and from our heart that we effect a "letting go" of resentment, bitterness, and painful experiences.

As I am writing this chapter on forgiveness, I must admit that I am no expert on the subject. I only know that I can't live without it. I know that I need the forgiveness of God each day in my life and it is urgent that I not deny it to others. When we hold unforgiving matters in our heart, it is like a poison that will cause serious spiritual illness. Forgiveness is necessary and if possible and under the right circumstances such matters must be dealt with. As we forgive and are forgiven, we are made whole; it is the story of restoration and reconciliation.

Anyone who takes the responsibility to seek forgiveness for their wrong actions and the painful experience they have brought on others is doing the Christ like thing. But this is not always so easily done; so while you are waiting for those who have hurt you to take the responsibility to come and apologize to you for their wrong actions, don't hold your breath. In waiting for them to make the first move, this may or may not ever happen. For this reason, you may continue to carry around the hurt, anger and resentment inside of you. Make peace with yourself and if possible with those who have hurt you; it is the Christian way to respond.

Anger will hold you back from having a spirit that is pleasing to God; we should resolve our problems as soon as possible. Jesus said this in Matt.5: 23, 24. "Therefore if thou bring thy gift to the altar, and there rememberest that thy brother hath ought against thee; leave there thy gift before the altar, and go thy way; first be reconciled to thy brother, and then come and offer thy gift." We are very hypocritical to say we love God while we hate others. The Word of God is clear on this: our attitudes toward others reflect our relationship with Him.

Anger is also a dangerous emotion that threatens to spring out of control. The longer we hold anger, grudges, bitterness, and resentfulness inside of us, the more likely that these ill feelings will turn into hate and maybe to violence. Emotional hurts can increase mental stress and broken relationships and can result in a violation of God's commandment to love. The test of our love for God is in how we treat others in response to how they have wronged us. It is understandable not to love the wrong behaviors of the person but we are to have a Christ love for them and to forgive them of their wrong that we may also be forgiven.

The Word of God instructs us to love our enemies, and do good to them who have wronged us. These are some powerful words to live by as we live the life of Christ, day by day. It is a reality that sometimes we are picked out by Satan to be picked on or to prove our faith and commandment to love. Satan will sometimes use those in whom we trust the most to hurt us or cause damage to our character or person in one way or another. The hurt and pain we may have encountered from others we have trusted in the past can be very difficult for us to forgive or even let go. But as Christ teaches us: we must forgive that we may be forgiven.

The question is this: can we truly forgive people who have really hurt and caused us pain, those in whom we have put our trust? Yes, but is this an easy thing to always do? No. But to obey the commandment of God to love, we must forgive those who have caused us emotional hurt and pain. Even the ones in whom we have trusted the most; that person we thought would never stoop so low to turn against us. We must forgive and let go of those ill feelings that we are holding inside--with the help of the Lord we will obey.

Most medical doctors will tell you that many health problems can occur by holding unforgiving, unresolved, emotional hurts inside of you. You can suffer from headaches, neckaches, backaches, stomachaches, and other pains, weight problems, or eat too much when emotionally upset. In addition to this, the chronic stress as a result of unresolved, unforgiving emotional hurts could contribute to serious health problems as well, such as hypertension, ulcers, cancers, and heart disease. The sooner we forgive ourselves and those who have wronged us, as well as resolve our conflicts, our relationship with God will be better, we will have peace within, and our health condition will improve and change for the better.

It is a fact that many people fall out of fellowship with one another when the wrong words are said due to differences of opinion. It is when people fall out of fellowship with each other that these ill feelings of grudges, resentment and bitterness begin to develop inside of them. Differences of opinion are inevitable among human personalities; at times, it could actually be helpful. When our differences are handled well with spiritual unity, they can be resolved in a peaceful and loving way. When we refuse to let spiritual unity take place in our lives, the ability to freely forgive someone and let go of a grudge will be a struggle to say the least.

To forgive is to let go and to free yourself of any ill feelings you may have against those who have wronged you. It has to be your personal decision to be true to yourself and in obedience to the Word of God in a continuous relationship with Him, to let go and forgive. There are some people who simply cannot, or will not, ever forgive in spite of the burden of emotional hurt and being in danger of the judgment of God. They carry around these painful thoughts:

"I will never forget them for what they did to me"
"I hate her; I want her to feel the pain she caused me"
"I hope he dies or something bad happens to him"

What we may fail to realize is when we refuse to let go of resentments, we are giving those ills feelings the authority to control our attitude, behavior and character. This will cause us to be in misunderstanding with others, unhappy, sacrificing our health and relationships. Bitterness, ill feelings and resentments of past hurts can also cause stress related symptoms, such as insomnia or interrupted sleep and upsetting dreams. The more we deny and guard these ill feelings of resentment, the more stress and health related symptoms we may be bringing upon ourselves. To say let it go and forgive can be easy to say when it is not you who is the victim. But to let it go and forgive is what we must do to free ourselves of the guilt and torment that we are struggling with. Remember if we don't forgive, neither will our heavenly Father forgive us.

Making peace means you have to
Give up something

Making peace with someone can sometimes be a challenge, but the process will bring to you a wonderful feeling of liberation and a lasting satisfaction. Learning to forgive from the heart is the key to personal growth and having a better understanding of relationship, and how to love and be loved. This is the teaching of Christ: to forgive and love them who have caused you hurt. The Lord holds us responsible for the ill feelings of resentment against someone that we are harboring inside of us. We have a responsibility to make a sound decision to release any and all ill feelings of resentment and liberate ourselves from the torment of it.

No one can really have peace of mind in making peace with others without giving up some things; you have to give up the anger, the resentments, the need to blame, and the desire to punish those who have hurt you. Sometimes you may suffer with a pain of hurt which is so deep that it becomes very difficult to forgive or let go, but making peace and giving up the resentment that you are holding inside of you are steps in the right direction for peace of mind.

Deep emotional wounds can be a major hindrance making it extremely difficult for some to openly forgive another who may have caused such pain. The hurt can be so overwhelming that bringing themselves to the point of forgiving may not be so easy. But we must not allow our hurt to become a hindrance to us from releasing all of our ill feelings and resentments. As previously stated, by holding these hurtful emotions inside, you may experience many stress related symptoms. You will discover that you are doing yourself a world of good if you release yourself of the stress; then your emotional healing can began to take place.

> Our words can heal or
> They can be destructive.

We should understand the danger of our tongue; a few words spoken in anger can destroy a relationship that took years to build. So before you speak, you must realize that words are like fire and you can neither control nor reverse (call back) the damage they can do. Damaging words can spread quickly and you cannot stop the consequences once they are spoken. To seek forgiveness later for the wrong you have caused will not remove the destruction that has been done. We sometimes speak words out in hurt and anger in the hope of making ourselves feel better not realizing we are making a bigger mess of the situation. Know that words used in the wrong way can pull a person down; they can destroy and, yes, even cause a death. Think before you speak. Ask yourself: Is this what I truly want to say? Is it necessary? Is it kind?

There are people who say careless words to hurt others thinking that they can apologize and seek their forgiveness later. Although they may forgive you, you must remember the scars you have caused remain. The Bible tells us in James 3: 6: "And the tongue is a fire, a world of iniquity: so is the tongue among our members, that it defileth the whole body, and setteth on fire the course of nature; and it set on fire of Hell." We need to realize that when we say hurtful and damaging words to hurt others, we are in danger of God's judgment. The careless words that we say to hurt someone out of anger can be just as bad as if we had used our own hands to take the person's life. Therefore, we are accountable for the things that come from our tongue; it is a small member of the body but can do great damage.

As you have been forgiven
You also forgive

Jesus gives an illustration (in Matt.18: 23-34) of a king who decided to bring his accounts up to date. In the process, one of his debtors was brought in to him who owed him approximately $3,000,000! He could not pay it, so the king ordered him to be sold for the debt along with his wife and children and everything he owned. But the debtor fell down before the king, and said, "Oh, king, be patient with me and I will pay it all." Then the king was moved with pity for him and released him and forgave him of his debt.

After the man was forgiven of his debt, he went to a man who owed him approximately $700.00. He grabbed him by the throat and demanded instant payment. The man fell down before him and begged him to give him a little time. He pleaded with him and said, "Be patient with me and I will pay it all." But the man would not hear of it. He had him arrested and put in jail until the debt was paid in full.

When this man's friends saw what he had done to the man that owed him, they went back and reported this to the king. The king called this man before him who he had forgiven of his debt and said, "You evil-hearted wretch! I forgave you all of that tremendous debt that you owed me just because you asked me to. Shouldn't you have mercy on others, just as I had mercy on you? Then the angry king sent the man to the torture chamber until he had paid every last penny due. Jesus tells us so shall our Heavenly Father do unto us if we refuse to truly forgive our brother.

Just as our loving and merciful God forgives us all our sins, we should not withhold forgiveness from others. When you really think about it and realize how freely Christ has forgiven us, it should generate a passionate attitude of forgiveness in us toward others. I must make reference to the Word again; the Word of God says that we are to forgive that we may be forgiven. If you do not forgive others of their trespasses neither will your Heavenly Father forgive you of your trespasses. Jesus not only taught frequently about forgiveness, He also demonstrated His own willingness to forgive. Here are just several examples that should be an encouragement to recognize His willingness to forgive us also.

The woman caught in adultery	John 8:3-11
The woman who anointed Christ feet with oil	Luke 7:47-50
Peter, for denying he knew Jesus	John 18:15-18, 25-27; 21:15-19
The thief on the cross	Luke 23:39-43
The people who crucified Him	Luke 23:34

Therefore, if we are not willing to forgive others, we become spiritual cripples and fall back into sin because God will not continue to forgive us. We must freely choose to forgive others if we are to get the forgiveness we so desperately need from our heavenly father. As we forgive others, a barrier between us and the Lord comes down and we begin to receive more and more of His loving forgiveness.

Forgiveness is the one gift we most need, both to give and receive. Each time we forgive it is a healing as God's love flows through us. Forgiveness is made possible by the forgiveness extended to us in Jesus Christ. When we refuse to forgive others, we are then setting ourselves above the ultimate sacrifice of Christ.

Chapter 7

Faith to Remove All Doubt

As I turn to my discussion on faith, I feel the only way to do justice to this subject is by writing a whole chapter rather than to just make mention of faith in other chapters in my book. Let us examine the benefits of faith along with its value. There is a well-rehearsed verse in the Bible with which we are very familiar because we have repeated many times. It relates to our test of faith or the ills of life we may find ourselves in at one time or another. The verse to which I am referring is found in Heb.11: 1. "Now faith is the substance of things hoped for, the evidence of things not seen."

With regard to this verse, I have a concern. Many people recite the verse just for the sake of showing they know it rather than as a conviction or affirmation of the verse. Strong belief is the actual existence of one's faith when one shows conviction in an absolute or positive stand. "Strong belief" is not just professing the word. When trouble comes into our lives, recitation of the words of the verse is not enough. Our actions and response in faith must speak louder than a well-rehearsed performance of the verse. As I so often say, true faith is found in action; faith without works is dead.

> Don't doubt God.
> He works miracles.

When we allow doubt to take control of our minds, we are making room for distrust, uncertainty, confusion, insecurity, and fear. We begin to ask "What if" questions like: What if God doesn't heal me? What if God can't fix my condition? What if I can't meet the needs and care of my children? The downside to this is as we continue to entertain doubt, it will mentally place a fixation of uncertainty in our minds. This will make it difficult for us to securely trust and believe in God concerning the circumstances in our lives. God is pleased when we trust in him; wavering results in doubt and unbelief. The bible tells us in Heb. 11:6: "But without faith it is impossible to please him" for he that cometh to God must believe that He is a rewarder of them that diligently seek him. We must strive to live by faith each day. Faith is a daily walk.

Doubt will paralyze your trust in God. Doubt will drain the energy of your faith; it will also deplete the resources of your patience. Doubt causes you to reside in fear and in the uncertainties of your circumstances. To believe God exists is the beginning of faith; but our faith must go further than that. Demons also believe in the existence of God. Our faith must be an active faith built with patience and trust in God who is the rewarder. An assured or true faith comes by having a personal life-transforming relationship with the Lord. When we diligently seek him, then we shall be rewarded with God's intimate presence. So what is faith? It is the assurance of things hoped for, the conviction of things not seen. Faith is the substance that goes against the visible.

Faith is keeping your eyes on the prize as a runner in a race. In spite of the trying temptations to quit or fall by the wayside, he refuses to let up until he crosses the finish line. Faith is perseverance and endurance. We don't lose heart; in the spiritual realm we throw off everything that hinders us. You see, tough faith is a true commitment to hanging on, trusting and believing God against all odds, no matter what. This what I call absolute faith. It is our confidence and trust in God's promises. The trials and suffering we have to endure are not joyful in themselves, but we must be joyful in them because of what the Lord is going to do through the testing of our faith.

It was after the Lord had filled me with the baptism of the Holy Ghost (Holy Spirit) that I began to develop a deeper understanding of faith and trust in Him than ever before. My faith was strong in the Lord, but after He had filled me with the Holy Ghost, my faith in Him became greater. During this time, my youngest son was about four years old. He had gotten an electric shock from a 240 watt outlet; the discharge was so great that it burned his hand, arm, and his bottom lip. As he was lying there on the floor with seventy percent of his bottom lip burned from his face, I realized that he was not breathing. I immediately ran over to him and starting praying. As I was praying and calling on the Lord, I also was trying to pump air back into his lungs. But it was not working. It is at moments like this that you have to reach deep into your faith.

We each must be firm in whom we believe. I myself have taken a stand: my hope is built on nothing or no one else than Jesus Christ. The conduct of my faith and trust is governed by the principles in which I believe. These principles do not permit alteration of course in my faith. We must stay focused on the promises of the Lord. I had to reach deep into my faith because I was facing a crisis: my son was lying on the floor and was not responding. My unyielding faith was in the God of my salvation. He who can do all things; there is nothing too hard for God.

Satan used this opportunity to try to weaken me. He came and began to speak to me telling me to give up because there was nothing anyone could do to help my son. But I rebuked Satan and that deceiving thought he was trying to put into my mind. His attempt was to get me to accept the spirit of doubt. I said to him, "Satan, you are a liar; you are not my doctor." I then began to call on the Lord in a more determined faith. I said, "Lord, only You can bring my son back. Father, you are my doctor. Put life back into his body." And, as I was there praying over my son with an inflexible faith, I want you to know that the Lord did come through for me. Without a doubt, the Lord put life back into my son's body and he began to breathe on his own. "Praise the Lord!"

My next test of faith was after I had taken my son to the children's hospital to have him examined by a doctor. After the doctors examined my son, the diagnosis was very good. It was what I had expected. My son was in good health; he did not sustain any other injuries from the electrical shock. The medical doctors remarked that this was nothing short of a miracle. Considering the type of accident my child had experienced, the doctors felt that my child is truly blessed because he is alive and has no brain damage. I need to say a word at this moment. It is this: **your faith is a light to others**. I have learned that when trouble comes and my faith is challenged, what will help me to determine how I am going to get through it is how I look at it.

After the doctors had completed their examination of him, I was told by the medical staff that it would be necessary for me to let my child stay in the hospital so they could perform surgery to restore his bottom lip. Well, at this time I was feeling victorious about the miracle the Lord had already performed on my son so it was easy for me to give them my decision. It was the Lord in whom I trusted so my reply to the medical staff was "no." I said to them that just as you all have said that his life was God's miracle, I am now going to look to God for another miracle.

I had no doubt that God is a healer; my faith was now stronger in Him than ever before. Once you have had a personal victorious experience with God, the kind of experience that you know could only come from Him, your faith then is complete in Him. I am speaking of the kind of experience where doubt cannot torment you. It is now hard for anyone to have you turn your faith and trust away from God. He is a miracle worker.

What you must understand is that strong faith is deep-rooted in the trust of God; it causes you to believe against all odds. Deep-rooted faith causes you not to stagger at the promise of God through unbelief. When you have strong faith in Him, it will cause you to give God the glory even in the midst of your troubles. Deep-rooted faith will also cause you to be fully persuaded in God, and in the things He has promised. Deep-rooted faith is your absolute assured trust in the promises of the Lord.

After refusing to allow the medical staff to perform surgery on my son, they informed me that social services would be visiting me. In the meantime, while the department of social services was doing their best to get me to bring my child into the hospital, I was confirming my faith in God through fasting and praying that He would restore my son's bottom lip. The stage was now set for God to show up in a supernatural way by performing another miracle on my son.

It was not easy while I waited for God to prove himself through the faith and trust that I have in Him. Satan was trying to distract me in every way. Satan is not going to leave you alone just because God has worked a miracle for you in the past. Satan is a deceiver who is going to work to destroy your faith in whatever way he can and in whom ever he can. He will come to you through your friends, loved ones, neighbors, or whom ever he can use to stir up doubt in your spiritual life. But you must stand strong as you are waiting knowing that because of your faith in God, your waiting will not be in vain.

My circumstances were not at all pleasant but my trust was in the Lord. In spite of the tribulations I was facing, I was waiting steadfastly on the Lord to complete His job. While waiting for another miracle, I was fasting and praying each day for the healing of my child. At times it was very frustrating for me. I received calls from people and others I did not even know. They said I was foolish to believe that God would heal my son's lip. Some of the calls I received were very emotionally upsetting to me, but this is how the Devil will work when he wants you to give up on God. Your faith will be tested. If you have a faith that cannot be tested, it cannot be trusted.

You must know that when your faith is being tested Satan is trying to destroy your confidence in God. Be aware, Satan will steal your joy, your healing and your victory. So you must get to know well the voice of the Lord; then you will be keenly aware of the Devil schemes, and you will then stay focused while in your wait. As I was waiting, my conviction was God would keep his promise. In job 13:14 b, it says: "All the days of my appointed time will I wait, till my change come." Now the key word here is "wait." Faith teaches us patience and through patience we have hope. There are times when you will have to wait, but the victory will come as you hold to your confident trust in the promises of the Lord.

While you are waiting on the Lord to work a miracle in your life, it is essential that you don't allow Satan to place fear in your heart. When you allow him to do that, doubt and apprehension creep into your life. Then doubt becomes fear and you begin to think that maybe God won't work a miracle in your life, maybe you are foolish to think that He can. When you give in to fear and doubt, thoughts of what people are saying about you will take over and weaken your resolve.

Fear is doubt and it will deprive you of purpose and victory, but through faith we endure our tests and trials victoriously as we reap the blessing of spiritual maturity. You see, as you await your break-through, you may need to stand and encourage yourself as you are speaking victory over your situations. Even if there is no one to stand with you, you must stand on your own faith. You must learn how to encourage yourself in the Lord by speaking the word of faith for yourself.

Life and death are in the power of the tongue, (Prov.18: 21). Life is what you want, so speak life; if you stand, the Lord will stand with you. As I was standing on the promises of God and waiting for Him to come through for me, I was then doing what the Bible tells us to do, that is, to rest in the Lord and wait patiently for Him. When we are resting in the Lord, we are allowing our faith to build in us, and we are not allowing room for the Devil to place doubt in our minds. Doubt is one of his tools of deception; we must understand that deception is the greatest weapon Satan has to use against us. If you give in to Satan's deception, he will mislead you from the truth of God. The deceiver will try to persuade you to believe that God does not hear your prayers. Satan will try to get you to believe that the Lord cannot help you in these kinds of circumstances. But God is truth, His word is true and He will do just what He promised. Remember your test of faith produces endurance.

In spite of my tribulations while I was waiting on the Lord to heal my son, my faith in Him was absolute. My trust was positive in whom I believe. My complete trust was in the healing power of the Lord. As your faith is being tested, rest in

His word. As I have stated in chapter 8 of my book, absolute faith is your positive stand in the Lord; it is your complete trust in Him. You are making a profound statement that your trust is in Him and Him only, not having your fingers crossed, or believing in some other alternative. Your absolute faith is holding on to the promises of the Lord; if God said it, He is faithful to perform it.

I am so blessed! Praise the Lord! My waiting was not in vain. The Lord came through for me; He kept his promise. **The Lord completely healed my son. "Bless His Holy name!"** If you put your trust in the Lord, it is your faith and trust that will move Him into action. I have learned how to build a foundation of trust in the Lord that comes only through fasting and prayer. Now I know for myself that the Lord is a healer; not only did He heal my son, but the Lord has also healed my body so many times. "Thanks be to God for His great healing power." You don't have to allow your circumstances to dictate your faith.

There is a song that I love to sing because the lyrics are in tune with my spirit. It was written by Edward Mote:

My hope is built on nothing less than Jesus' blood and righteousness?
I dare not trust the sweetest frame, but wholly lean on Jesus' name
On Christ, the solid rock, I stand; all other ground is sinking sand,
All other ground is sinking sand.

When darkness veils his lovely face, I rest on his unchanging grace;
In every high and stormy gale, my anchor holds within the veil. On
Christ, the solid rock, I stand: all other ground is sinking sand, all
Other ground is sinking sand.

As I speak to you on faith, I recall a surgical procedure that was scheduled for me by my primary physician. I don't mind telling you that at the time I was afraid to go through with it. But I thought of the God whom I serve, and it was at that moment I decided to trust in the Lord for my healing. I appealed to the Lord to heal my body and turned my condition over to Him. Upon informing my family and medical doctor of my decision to trust completely in the Lord for my healing, my faith was established. Faith must be acted upon, tell somebody what God will do, and put the Devil to open shame. (He has put us to shame too many times.) Put your trust in the Lord and be ye steadfast.

I don't want anyone to misunderstand me in my writing on this chapter of faith. Undoubtedly, I give much credit to medical science and the wonderful work our medical professionals are doing around the world. I encourage anyone, if you have a medical need or think that you do, to seek professional medical attention if you do not have the faith you need in God for your healing.

I am so encouraged in the Lord. During troubling times, I have put my trust in the Lord and on His promises and He has never let me down. I believe anytime the Lord speaks to your spirit to trust Him, which is comforting, it is His promise of victory to you. Your absolute patience and faith in His promise will give you victory; He can do what no other power can do.

These are the words of faith my mother would speak concerning her steadfastness in the Lord: "You can't make me doubt him; I know too much about him." And now I can speak those same words of faith for myself: "You can't make me doubt him, I know too much about him." When you know without a doubt what the Lord can do, it gives you the assurance in faith.

An assured faith is our
absolute trust in Him.

Elder G. E. Johnson

An assured faith believes against all doubts; it is the unshaken adherence; it is absolute, independent of and unrelated to anything else. When we learn by trusting in God how to have an assured faith, we will be able to speak to our troubles and they will be removed from our life. Having an assured faith is unfailing trust in the Lord; it is the kind of trust where hope still reigns in our heart even as men open up the grave. To have assured faith in God is also the conviction of our mind fixed in strong belief that He is a rewarder of our faith.

As I have stated earlier, your faith moves God into action; His ears are open to our cry. Many times my faith has enlightened me in advance of trouble, sickness, and other evil works that Satan was sending my way to torment me. But due to my assured faith in God and unfailing trust in Him, often I am able to speak with authority against the will of Satan and send his evil works back to the pits of hell. Through faith, the Lord gives us power to speak victory over our circumstances, power over all of the works of the evil one.

Faith is our absolute confident belief in God; this is when our belief rests in Him and not in logical proof or material evidence. Our faith believes against all doubts. Doubt will stop the progress of your healing and deliverance; when we doubt God, we are telling Him that we don't believe He is able to help us in our situation. Therefore, we lose all hope of a satisfying result. In my many experiences of trusting the Lord in tough situations, I find myself believing in Him to do even greater things for me. We can stand on the promise of God and declare our healing and deliverance. The unfailing trust we have in Him is our assured faith at work; it gives us the confidence to have the boldness to speak with an authority against everything the Devil is trying to bring against us.

When we are in the midst of a test and trying to confront our trials from a human perspective, we are going to get very discouraged. But when we see our trials from a spiritual or eternal angle, our spirit is then renewed for victory. We have our example of patience and endurance in trials that is Jesus Christ Himself. In Hebrews 12:2, it tells us how Jesus endured the cross as He looked past His trials to the victory that awaited Him. It is the way in which we look at our trials that will help us in determining how we will make it. The Bible tells us to count our trials as joy. Our joy is spiritual, but it has an internal well-being regardless of the things that may be happening externally.

Fasting and prayer
Is necessary

In my discussion on the subject of "faith to remove all doubt," it would be remiss of me if I did not include the necessary topic of fasting and prayer. Fasting and prayer is and should be a very important part of all our lives. Faith needs prayer for its development and growth, and prayer needs fasting for the same reason. Fasting will do wonders for you when practiced in combination with prayer and faith.

Satan will place so many temptations in our lives that only a good prayed up life of fasting and prayer will help to defeat him. In order for us to be strong in our faith in God, we must have a good prayer life that includes fasting. Prayer is the avenue to which we have direct communication with God and He with us. In speaking on prayer, Christ said that man should always pray and not to faint. In other words, don't give up, wait on the Lord, wait I say on the Lord.

Fasting humbles the soul before God; it manifests earnestness before Him to the exclusion of all else and shows obedience. Our fasting demonstrates the mastery of our will over appetite. When we are fasting, it gives us victory over temptation and helps keep us in line with the will of God. Along with these benefits, it manifests strength and growth in our faith. Fasting and prayer will help us to attain power over demons, and will benefit us in developing a strong faith and belief in the working powers of God. Our fasting crucifies unbelief and aids us in prayer and faith. You see, through faith, fasting and prayer, you are able to build a good foundation of trust and assurance in God; if you call on Him, He will answer.

Finally, we have a God who is faithful in His promise. He is a God who does not lie, and He is the only absolute, positively trustworthy God. Find that place in Him that your faith will be established. The more we trust God through faith, the more victories; the more victories, the less doubts; the less doubts, the greater your faith will be. Remember, He is faithful.

Chapter 8

Be Healed, be Delivered, and be Set Free

"Be healed, be delivered, and be set free." I have attentively listened to the beloved late Bishop G. E. Patterson as he spoke these powerful words of faith while preaching the Word of God. The preaching of the Word of God is a blessing to my soul. Dear hearts, you don't have to wait until you have enough faith to be blessed. A little faith can move mountains, so build up yourself on the "now faith" that you have. The longer you wait for greater faith to believe, the weaker your faith becomes; but if you believe right now, and act now upon the faith you do have, the stronger your faith will become. In other words, build on what you have. You can be blessed now as you receive these words of God by faith: *"Be healed, be delivered, and be set free."* If you believe, you shall receive.

When we allow ourselves through faith to take hold of the promises of God, the mighty power of God is released into action on our behalf and we are blessed. It is my sincere belief that the Lord is a complete deliverer from all hurts and ills of life. I believe His healing can make us whole in our bodies, in our soul, mind and spirit, even in our relationships, attitudes, and way of life. His healing sets us free, but our faith in Him must be based on love. We must have a personal, active faith in the Lord for our healing, because mental faith alone is not enough nor is positive thinking. You must believe that God's will is for you to be healed, delivered and set free, and then act upon it to be (complete) made whole.

Do you believe?

My hope for all is that you do believe "God is a healer." I know that He is! This is not what someone has told me, my friend, but it is from my personal life experiences of faith and trust in the Lord. The Lord can and will heal you right now; regardless of the condition you are presently in. If you call on that name "Jesus" and believe that He can, and will, whatever your condition is in life, you will be healed, delivered, and set free. Jesus will give sight to the blind, open up deaf ears, make the lame walk, yes, Jesus can call the dead back to life. Everything is possible with the Lord. But it is so important for you to believe in whom you are calling on for your deliverance. Do you believe Jesus Christ is the Son of God? In the Bible we find these words: "…I am come that they might have life and that they might have it more abundantly" (John 10:10). God sent His son Jesus Christ into the world that through Him, we might have an abundant life.

Putting your faith in action

The Bible tells us of a woman who was very sick, and she had been sick for twelve years. This woman had gone to many doctors but they could not cure her. She had an "issue of blood' and was not in good health. One day, she heard of Jesus and His healing power, and began to speak these words of faith within herself: "If I can but touch the hem of His garment I shall be made whole." As she was speaking the words of faith, believing and acting on it, she was healed. Her act of faith brought her in harmony with the Lord to be healed. Instantly, she was cured of her malady (disease). Jesus said to the woman, "Thy faith hath made thee whole." Having "absolute faith" and acting upon it, she was able to tap into the healing power of Christ. By putting her faith in action, her life was made whole.

The point I must make here is this: the Lord seeks to give man a more abundant life. While people are struggling with sickness, pain, fear, and other ills in life, they need to know that God's will for them is to have an abundant life. You will find in Him full healing power, and He is ready to set you free. As the late Bishop G. E. Patterson would say, "When the Lord heals you, He tells you to go in peace, thy faith hath made thee whole, and sin no more." And this is the good news: there is no need for anyone to become submissive to the pressures in life nor the antagonism and malice of the Devil. The Lord is able to give you healing and deliverance form the oppressions of the evil one and all his angels. You see God wants us to have a full life, to be made whole, as we live our lives responsible unto Him.

It is the will of God that our lives be changed through His son Jesus Christ, to live responsible unto Him; we continue to use our faith to achieve victory even as we encounter the ills of life. "God is able to make all grace abound in you, so that you always having all sufficiency in everything, you may have an abundance for every good deed" (2 Cor. 8:8). God's ever-active concerns for His people are manifested in His ready love and promise to help us in time of trouble.

Receive your healing and deliverance now. You may be suffering from some kind of sickness or disease even at this very moment; you may feel like giving up and your hope has come to an end. You don't have to fear. I want you to know that God cares for you. It is not over for you no matter what anyone tells you. It is not over until God says it is over. It is in Him we live, we move, and we have our being, He gives us life and our lives can be taken by Him, or our lives can be healed be Him. Why don't you reach out and touch Him right now! Have you really talked to Him lately?

Don't be afraid to trust God because you can be healed at this very moment. Fear will hinder you from releasing your faith to be healed. Fear is torment, it is destructive to your faith, and without faith you can't please God. As you seek Him, You must believe that He is a rewarder. You must be keenly aware of the presence of the Lord, and truly believe that He is right there where you are right now to meet your every need. As you release your faith and act upon it, you can be set free from the powers of sickness, disease, and fear. God's grace is available for us all to be healed and made whole. He forgives all iniquities and heals all our diseases.

Receive ye the Lord!

The Bible tells us that we should bless the Lord, and magnify His Holy name, to make His praise glorious, and all that is within us to bless His Holy name. He is so worthy to be praised. Psalm 34:8 tells us "…blessed is the man that trusteth in Him." Our trust should be continually in the Lord, whatever your circumstances are in life. In 1.Peter 5:7, the Word of God tells us to cast all of our cares upon Him, for He careth for us. Satan hates the fact that we can pray to God for ourselves. Through prayer, you have the advantage over Satan, and your communion with God through faith gives you the power and strength to overcome temptation and adversity. "Let us therefore come boldly unto the throne of grace, that we may obtain mercy and find grace in time of need." (Heb. 4:16).

The Lord will grant your petition through faith, as you give Him reverence and praise so, yes, you can receive your deliverance and be made whole. He will forgive you of your sins, heal your body and set you free from the oppression of the Devil. Sin and sicknesses, both mental and physical, are oppressions of the Devil. Peter tells us this in Acts 10:38: "… God anointed Jesus of Nazareth with the Holy Ghost and with power, who went about doing good, and healing all that were oppressed of the Devil for God was with him." Are you oppressed? Do you want to be made whole? The advantage you have over the oppressions of the Devil is that Jesus stands ready to set you free. Be encouraged and know that it is a blessing and a privilege to have such a benefit.

Beloved, receive Christ into your soul as your Lord and savior. Allow the healing virtue of the Lord to enter your sick body that you may be made whole. For He says: Behold I stand at the door and knock; if any man hear my voice, and open the door, I will come in to him, and will sup with him, and he with me. (Rev.3: 20.) Check Jesus is saying to you, "Here I am." He is waiting for you to open up the door of your heart. Do it now and let Christ into your life that you may be made whole. When we accept Christ as our Lord and savior, we begin to live a responsible life unto Him and we give way for our faith to take hold of the promises of the Lord. Therefore, beloved, by the power of God through faith, you can decree your healing and deliverance. The Lord is honored in our faith by answering the prayers of believers.

Be mindful of the saying that what a man thinks, so is he. If you send out a certain thought pattern continually, you are likely to receive the same thought pattern. In Mark 11: 23, we find these words of the Lord: "For verily I say unto you, that whosoever say unto this mountain, be thou removed, and be thou cast into the sea, and shall not doubt in his heart, but shall believe that those things which he saith shall come to pass, he shall have whatsoever he saith." Let us learn how to project good outcomes in our minds. You see, if you anticipate a bad outcome or destructive results, you are more likely to receive them. Therefore, with the same principle, if you anticipate a good outcome, you will receive it.

Absolute Faith for Your Healing

Absolute faith in your healing will bring you positive results. If you project a continuous faith pattern of healing and deliverance, your results will be good. I had a very dear friend who lived to be over a hundred years old. He was my mentor and a preacher of the gospel. He lived on his own and cared for himself. He was a man who was full of faith and lived a life in fellowship with God. He has made that great transition to be with the Lord. He took ill when he was about eighty-seven years old. He was in poor health, his blood pressure was dangerously low, and the prognosis of his condition was not good at all. In spite of all this, he exemplified absolute faith in his healing. He projected in his mind a continuous faith pattern of healing in his body. He would speak words of faith and healing which reflected a profound belief in the healing power of God.

Here is what was remarkable and magnificent about my friend's healing: it is the fact that in spite of how painful and weak his ravaged body was, he would not allow him mind to settle to the condition of his body. Instead, he tuned out his misery and the unfavorable reports he received from the doctor, and focused on God's healing virtue as it moved through his body. He had the faith to sense the presence of God bringing deliverance to his body in spite of his deteriorating health condition.

This is a man who was well up in age and by all accounts his sickness should have taken his life, but he refused to permit his mind to think that his condition was irreversible or he was too old to live any longer. This hero of faith did not give in to any of these discouraging factors to tarnish or diminish his faith. He would speak healing daily by saying, "I feel the presence of the Lord upon me now as He is bringing healing throughout my body; I am being healed now, I praise God for His healing power."

Even as my friend was lying in his bed in pain, he prayed and gave glory to God. As he spoke the words of faith, he would say: "The Lord's healing virtue is entering into my body now; I am being healed by the power of God." Then he would begin to give God praise for his healing. The result of his absolute faith in the healing power of God was good; my dear friend received complete healing in his body, he made a full recovery. The Lord healed his body and made him whole. He was my friend and mentor who lived to be a hundred and one years old.

If you have absolute faith and anticipate a good outcome, give praise to God in advance, remove doubt from your heart, and you will produce the kind of faith that will give good results. So pray, believe continuously, and leave your deliverance to the Lord. By faith, your outcome will be good.

Absolute faith will give you confidence to be healed, even when the doctor tells you that, based on all of his test results, you will never be able to walk again. But you can speak to the doctor and tell him that, based on the results of all of your tests of faith, you know that you will walk again. Or the medical doctor may say to you, based on all of his years of experience and knowledge, the condition that you have cannot be reversed. But with confidence through absolute faith, you can say to the medical doctor that, based on your experience and knowledge of God's healing power, you know that you can be healed, delivered and set free of your condition. No matter how critical the condition may be, God has the power to reverse your troubles to good and favorable results.

Absolute faith will give you confidence to speak boldly. Another point to be made here is this: as we abide in Him and He in us, our confidence will cause our faith to line up with the will of God. Therefore, Jesus tells us: "If you abide in me and my word abides in you, you can ask what you will and it shall be done." The Lord is saying that if our abiding faith meets the conditions for our asking, we shall receive.

When I speak of "absolute faith," I am speaking of being steadfast without wavering in what you believe. Absolute faith in God is a complete and unconditional trust in Him. You see, when we have this kind of faith in God, you don't go around with your fingers crossed at the same time. Absolute faith in God is independent of and unrelated to anything else, so it is in Him and Him alone in whom we must put our trust.

Praise God in advance for deliverance. Remember the Bible tells us that faith is the substance of things hoped for, and the evidence of things not seen. You must believe in the Lord with an assured faith for your deliverance, while praising Him in advance. Just because you don't see results immediately, that does not mean that the Lord is not taking care of it. Satan grabs this opportunity to test your faith because you are trusting without being able to see with the natural eye who you are trusting in. God is a spirit, and they that worship Him must worship Him in spirit and in truth.

The Lord does not only deliver you from sickness and other things in life that Satan tries to bind us down with, but He is God who will deliver us out of trouble as well. I want you to be encouraged knowing that God is a present help in time of trouble. He will allow you to rest in His supernatural presence at that moment or period in time of your deliverance. There will be particular times and situations in our lives when we need the Lord to answer our prayers and deliver us. It is for this reason that we should have a good prayer life; as believers, we should pray when things are going well and when trouble arises.

There will be times in your life when you will need to already have some prayers stored up in Heaven, because situations do arise when you are unable or don't have the time to pray. I have found myself in dire situations when all I could do or had time to do was call on that name "Jesus!!" It is for this reason I am propelled to advise you that it is a personal advantage over your troubles to have a good prayer life.

As I look back on one of my unforgettable experiences many years ago, I am so blessed to say how thankful I am to God who is faithful. This was one of those situations where I needed God to deliver me instantly, at that very moment and time as I previously stated. I can say to you without a doubt that He is a present help in time of trouble, and He was just that kind of help for me.

About fifteen years ago, I was involved in a very scary situation as I was traveling on I-20 E. just outside of Atlanta, Ga. I was en route to a little town called Monroe, Ga. located about fifty miles outside of Atlanta to attend a church service. As I was driving east on the interstate, out of nowhere came this big eighteen-wheeler truck pulling two large trailers. The driver was speeding and the truck seemed to be out of control because the driver appeared to be having difficulty trying to stay in his lane.

As this driver sped recklessly around me, he attempted unsuccessfully to cut in between my car and the car in front of me. He misjudged the distance between the two cars. As the second trailer that was being pulled by the truck came around me, the rear end of the trailer violently hit the front part of my car. The impact broke off my front wheel, thereby causing my vehicle to roll over three times on the interstate. My windshield and rear glass were also broken out from the impact.

As my vehicle was rolling over and over again and sliding down the interstate, most of the top part of the vehicle crushed in and the left front door popped off. While this destruction was taking place, I had no time to go into a long prayer but thank God I have a good prayer life and there were prayers in store. At that moment, when the trailer attached to that truck hit my car just before it began to roll over, I only had time to call on the name of Jesus!!! **I want you to know that there is power in the name** "**Jesus.**"

Another small piece of advice: always wear your seatbelt when you are driving. I was not wearing my seatbelt, but fortunately I was able to hold on to the seat of the car. The Lord held me in a safe position while the vehicle was rolling over and sliding upside down. Only the power of the Lord could have held me safely in the midst of that destruction because I had no seatbelt on and the door had popped off. At least three vehicles swerved off the road to avoid hitting me, and others were directed around me by the Lord. Once the destruction had come to an end, I got out of my car completely unhurt.

Note: it is well-reported that seat belts save lives; everyone should always be fastened securely and safely in them.

I wear glasses and, in spite of my car flipping over and over, my glasses were still on my face unbroken. In addition, there was no damage to my suit, shirt and tie. The Lord had taken good care of me. After the accident, many people came up to me expressing the fear that I was dead from the wreck. One lady came over to me and said that she had to just touch me because she knew the angel of the Lord was with me. In spite of the seriousness of that accident, there were no cuts or bruises on any part of my body, none at all.   I give all praises to God. The Bible tells us in Psa. 34:7: "The angel of the Lord encampeth round them that fear him, and delivereth them." If you put your trust in God, He will deliver you from all your troubles.

Blessed is the man or woman who put their trust in the Lord. I can tell you that if your faith is in Him, trouble can be all around you but God will not allow any of it to harm you. Psa. 91:11 states: "For He shall give His angels charge over thee, to keep thee in all thy ways." Do you not know that the Lord is wonderful and worthy to be praised? Do you have faith to believe?

The Lord is moved by our faith; it causes Him into action on our behalf, as we believe, through faith, our prayers are being answered. You may not be able to feel it or can't see it in the natural, but you must believe and praise Him in advance for what He is doing, and going to do, with an assured faith, giving Him the glory. Your assured faith of praise in advance will open unto you the blessing of the Lord. He is an ever-active concerned God who cares for you; therefore, we can take all our sickness, our troubles and cares unto Him. So release your faith now, by praising God in advance for your deliverance.

By trusting in the Lord I learned a long time ago that you don't have to wait until your spiritual battle is over to praise the Lord, but you can give Him praise and thanks now. You can do it now in the midst of your troubles, knowing that God is a healer, who can and will heal you from all sins and sickness, so that you may be made whole. Praise Him! For He will deliver you, "And call upon me in the day of trouble: I will deliver thee, and thou shall glorify me." (Psa. 50: 7.) Praise Him! He will set you free. "If the Son therefore shall make you free, you shall be free indeed." John: 8 36. You see, praising God in advance is the key to the expectation of a good outcome. We should give Him thanks and praise for what He has done for us, because when we look back over our lives there is so much we should be thankful for.

Don't fail to give praises to God for the things he has done for you already, and then praise him for what he is doing now. Do you not know that the Lord is blessing you right now in spite of your circumstances? Then give him praise for the blessings he is sending your way; thank him for the doors he is opening up for you now. The Lord has many good things in store for us, we just have to believe it and receive. And we must not forget to give the Lord praise and thanks for who He is; He is the God of all creation, the great "I Am." So whatever your needs may be, He is our God who shall supply all of our needs according to his riches in glory by Christ Jesus. This is the kind of trust that says "Yes, Lord, I believe." Give Him thanks and praise always.

Do you want to be made whole? I pray to God that your answer is yes; then receive ye Christ now as your Lord and savior. It is a choice that you must make; it is a critical step that has always been up to us. As you allow the Lord, through faith, to make you whole, you are then free to be more effective in the kingdom. We then live a holy life unto the Lord, for it is vital that we understand that holiness comes with our growing relationship with God. Holiness concerns itself with the quality of our lives, as to who we are, where we are and where we are going.

Be ye holy because I am holy. 1 Peter 1:16. There is a goal. Completeness: Christ came to make us whole and holy. One of the best ways to describe holiness is that it's not a state to be attained but a never-ending process. Holiness is a spiritual journey: we abiding in Christ, and He in us. It is not a place, a thing, or a building. It is the core of our continually growing relationship with and through Christ. Do you know that the word "salvation" comes from the Latin root word *salus*, which means wholeness? God is concerned with all of me and all of you. He cares about all our needs, intellectual, physical, emotional as well as our spiritual needs. The Lord is committed to the whole person. Therefore, we need to pursue, discover and develop our life of wholeness and holiness in Christ.

So, yes, you can be healed, be delivered and set free from whatever your problems in life may be. You don't have to be bound by sin, by your fears nor by the circumstances of your life. God is omnipotent. The Lord will make you whole. The Lord responds to your passionate appetite of faith. Faith moves God into action. Without faith you cannot please the Lord, but believe in Him with unwavering faith in spite of your circumstances. He will respond to your faith. Do you have a passion to be made whole? Is there a need you have in your life today? **Try Jesus!**

CHAPTER 9 ——————————————————————

AN ATTITUDE ADJUSTMENT

Allow me to begin this chapter in my discussion by asking several questions on the above subject matter: (1) How is your personality: is it sociably unappealing?

(2) Do you get along well with others? (3) Do people have to be very careful around you, even your own family members? (4) Is there someone to whom you owe an apology, but your pride and selfishness will not allow you to do it? Finally, (5) Do you always blame others for events and situations, for your misery, depression, and sadness? …If your answer is "yes" to any of the above questions, **you need an attitude adjustment**.

Are you happy and at peace with yourself? Your attitude is the manner in which you carry or conduct yourself. It dictates your mood and your state of mind. It is the people in our lives who bring us the most happiness. Family, friends, and co-workers, who are part of our inner circle, are the ones who share our experiences, our hopes and dreams, successes and failures, our joy and pain. Too often too many people take each other for granted.

It is my hope that, after reading this chapter, you will discover an informative principle for change in your life. As you begin to read, bear in mind these two questions: Do I need an attitude adjustment? Do I have the courage to change?

Happiness is probably the most elusive emotion and the most difficult to define. It is probably one of the easiest emotions to feel. Happiness comes to us as a direct result of positive self-worth, personal attitudes, specific actions, and an essential principle in behavior connected to the way in which we relate to other people. And one can say that happiness is the gratitude and appropriate behavior of us all as human beings and how it fits into our life process.

As I go through my daily life, I am so amazed to see so many people who seem to be unhappy. These are people who go through life as though they have a big chip on their shoulder which says "No one must come near me today." It appears that they are angry at the world and everything around them. People who have a bad attitude, which is a personal problem for them, sometimes fail to realize that they are their own worst enemy. They are unaware of the many hindrances in life they are creating for themselves. So often those who display a bad attitude may find it hard to maintain good employment because they don't take orders well from others. Neither do they cooperate with their co-workers. People who display such an attitude just might fail to grasp that, at various times in their life, their behavior becomes a hindrance to them in more ways then they could ever have realized. They will learn that problems will surface in friendships, relationships and true love. They will have difficulty socializing with people on the whole.

The most powerful tool that Satan uses against us is the spirit of deception. Satan's desire is to deceive you into thinking that you have no problem at all, and the problem is always with everyone else, not you. This causes you to harbor a spirit of deception imbedded in the disposition of selfishness, which will prevent you from socializing with people in a Christ like manner. We have so much to be thankful for in spite of the trials of life that we all must experience from time to time. One of numerous things I appreciate about the Lord is that he is there to help us in the difficult times of our lives. He will never fail you because he is a God who is faithful to his Word. Therefore, we should not allow ourselves to be fooled by Satan, but be thankful for new mercies and blessings that the Lord sends us each day. Also, those who have a lot of drama in their lives are allowing Satan to deceive them with a disagreeable disposition in attitude.

What we must understand about Satan is that his goal is to mislead you into wrong deeds, actions and thoughts. The price we pay when we allow ourselves to be misled by him is that he will spiritually blind you from the truth of God. Therefore, you are then permitting Satan the opportunity to deposit deadly emotions of ills and resentful feelings inside of you. Anyone who has these deadly emotions festering inside of them cannot enjoy the presence of the Lord nor can they benefit from the spiritual realm of God.

Deadly emotions can be described as spiritual torment; spiritual torment can affect your mind, body and soul. These emotions will affect you mentally by becoming a barrier which hinders you from truly being happy or at peace. Deadly emotions will also affect you physically to the point that it can become hazardous to your health. They may result in various ills such as hypertension, stomachaches, headaches, and possibly contribute to cancer. Lastly, these deadly emotions will affect you spiritually; as previously stated, these emotions will create a barrier that will prevent you from benefiting from the spiritual realm of God.

Elder G. E. Johnson

Be thankful

Each morning as we are blessed to wake up (and it is a blessing), we should be so thankful for the new day and a new start in life God has granted us. We should rise each new morning with our mind set to do good in this day that God have given us, and do well unto others. Let us live each day as though it is our last and it is the fact of life to us all. So if we are to make the best of each day that we are blessed with on this earth we should begin with a good attitude. A good attitude will carry you very far in life. Here are some words of commonsense my mother shared with me as a life lesson: "Son, always carry yourself in a decent and respectable way and have a good attitude about yourself as well, because where you are trying to go in life, your attitude will get there far before you will." I am so thankful for my mother and all of her wonderful words of wisdom. Although she has gone to be with the Lord, her wisdom and teaching shall continue to be a part of my understanding in life. I am truly grateful.

We should realize that in this life things are not always going to go well for us. However, in spite of the problems, we should always be thankful. **There are people at this very moment who are experiencing troubles and trials in their lives who are in far worst situations than you or I can comprehend; they would be most grateful to trade places with any of us.** When we earnestly think of the goodness of God and all of His benefits to us, we cannot help but be thankful. God is so good! In the Holy Bible we see how King David responded to the circumstances in his life even when there were men trying to kill him. King David responded with an attitude of gratefulness, "This is the day that the Lord has made, I will rejoice and be glad in it." You may be having a bad day, but because of whom you know (which is Jesus) and whose you are, there should be joy on the inside.

Life is filled with choices. We can choose to have a good attitude, we can choose to be bitter or we can choose to be better. Each time something bad happens, we can choose to be a victim or we can choose to learn from it. Every time someone comes to you complaining, you can choose to accept their complaint or you can point out the positive side of life. Life is about choices. When you get down to it, every situation presents a choice. You choose how you react to situations. You choose how people affect your mood. You choose to be in a good mood or a bad mood. It is your choice how you choose to live your life.

One of the greatest causes of unhappiness is self-pity. It can absolutely immobilize us from any action that may bring us happiness. There are people who lose much needed sleep, crying day and night, about things that have happened in their life that they can't change. To wallow in self-pity is to play the victim. Sometimes in this life friends and family disappoint us. There may be people who don't love us the way we think they should, or events and plans don't work out as we expected it to. What we should understand is that when you surrender to disparity and depressions, you are spiritually dying. We should learn from those situations and go on with our lives. These disappointments and failures threaten our sense of security, self-worth or pride. There are many people who respond negatively by allowing their behavior to become sociably unappealing. You alone are responsible for your attitude; your troubles don't have to determine your behavior.

People who go through life with a bad attitude are sacrificing intended blessings, friendships, relationships and favors. They are also sacrificing their future of much good that could be realized because they lack understanding of the crucial principle of 'people needing people.' We need the love and care of each other; my father would often say, "If nothing else, it's just nice to be nice." In a word, be virtuous. Virtue is a chain of all perfections, the center of all happiness. She makes you prudent, discreet, shrewd, sensible, wise, brave, cautious, honest, happy and praiseworthy, a true universal hero. Anyone who exhibits sociably unappealing behavior is establishing a pattern of negative collective character which is the opposite of virtue. Therefore, the negative characteristic that you display of yourself is the way others perceive you. While you are exposing yourself in a negative way, you are exhibiting a distinctive character trait or the typical person you are. You are also allowing your bad and unwanted behavior to be imbedded into the minds of others.

There are three things that will cause anyone to be blessed, a saint, wisdom, and prudence. Living a virtuous life wins God's grace and that of others. On the other hand, a negative attitude could become ingrained in our character. Our goal should be to eliminate such a thing. To do this, the first step is to be honest with ourselves. We must not make excuses and be pretentious by saying we see no faults in our character. Not accepting our shortcomings is what has fostered our bad behavior in the first place. One who displays bad character can cause many problems in life.

People who have a bad attitude and despicable character traits should realize that, in the time of need, their unsavory character could cause their cry of need to go unheard. Sometimes, the decision of others to respond and lend a helping hand in time of necessity just might be based on the collective negative character that has been imbedded in their minds concerning you. Therefore, a person's attitude and behavior can cause others to refrain from assisting them at a time of need. Sociably unacceptable behavior can have serious consequences in more ways than one can imagine. A bad attitude could cause others to suffer, especially family members who depend on our care. In short, your bad and unwanted attitude can wreak havoc in your life, as well on the members of your family.

Control your tongue

People who have an attitude problem generally discover that they also have a greater problem with their tongue. The bible tells us the tongue is a little member in the body but can be deadly. It says that it is easier to tame a horse than it is for some people to tame their tongue. The tongue is a little member of the body but can do damaging and destructive things. "It setteth on fire the course of nature, and defileth the whole body."

Each of us should realize that anyone with an attitude behavior is influenced by Satan. This problem is caused by his deceptive power to influence you to yield or submit yourself to his evil desires. But you have to allow yourself to be deceived by his evil influences. Satan can manifest his evil ways in us through our attitude, character and behavior only if we submit to his evil temptations. Having said that, the way and manner in which we carry ourselves in life is important. We need to know that our life is an open book to the public. Our character is on public display each day, therefore we should realize our actions and words will all point to the careless disposition of our character. Our behavior and character can come back in life to harass us as a thorn in our flesh.

We should be aware at all times that the action of an uncontrolled tongue can do untold damage to one's reputation. Satan also uses the tongue to divide people and put them against one another. Too many people who have a bad disposition do not think before they speak and their verbal carelessness becomes like a deadly poison. Here are some words of wisdom: "Even when you quarrel, you do it in such a way that you can make up."

Self-centeredness

Most people who are suffering with bad attitude behavior are struggling from within; it is the struggle of self-centeredness and the love of self. Many of them fail to understand that love of self and self-centeredness are not the same. If you love yourself and you are comfortable with whom you are, you will have no desire to display a bad and unwanted attitude toward others. But for those of us who have a problem of self-centeredness which manifests itself in a bad attitude, this can be overcome with a concerted effort to change the unwanted behavior. You must make a conscious decision to see yourself as God sees you; the goal here is to see yourself as you really are. You must be truthful with yourself in ways that you have overlooked in the past. You must conduct an honest self-examination, accept your faults and take steps in the right direction for change.

One might consider the question of intelligence: If I am intelligent, isn't that good enough? The answer is no, not at all. Our intelligence is not enough; we must be of good character as well.

The wisdom of old tells us that in order to display your true gift, there must be good character as well as intelligence. One without the other brings only part of success. It isn't enough to be intelligent; you must also have the right character. The wisdom of old will also tell you that the fool fails by behaving without regard to his condition, position, origin, or friendships.

Failure to recognize and accept your true behavior and character could result in a spirit of selfish pride. Pride in this case is an unreasonable conceit in a person; now the Bible tells us that a man's pride shall bring him down. And also Proverbs 16:18 reads: "Pride goeth before destruction and a haughty spirit before a fall." It is said and understood that most people who act with selfish pride unequivocally have an excessively high opinion of themselves. It is also understood that their deportment can be a hindrance to recognizing their problem is a need for change.

Now the difference in one who is not conceited is humbleness, a virtue which displays high morals, righteousness, goodness and accepting and taking responsibility. You see, if one wants to change a bad attitude behavior problem, there must be self-knowledge of one's shortcomings, accepting them and taking the responsibility to work through for change. In this life, each of us is responsible for our own behavior, or, permit me to say, our attitude, therefore the responsibility is upon us to hold ourselves accountable for our actions.

Be accountable for your
Actions

A lesson that was well learned when I was a little child is this: accept and take responsibility for your own actions. I can recall as a child playing in the front yard of our home with my brothers and sisters (those were some wonderful times and family life was good back in those days). My mother would be in the kitchen cooking and it seemed like we could not wait to all get around the dinner table as a family during dinner time.

Now one day, we were playing in the yard. My mother came to the front door as she always did and firmly reminded us to stay in our own yard and not venture off the premises. As usual, we agreed to do as we were told. But, on this particular day, my two brothers and I decided to go down the street around the corner to play with our friends in their yard. We decided to disobey and go where we wanted to go. "After all," we thought, "What harm could be done in going to play with our friends?" About a half an hour later, my mother found my brothers and me playing with our friends in their yard. She took us home and put us on punishment, saying, "You all must now take responsibility for your actions and the choice you made in disobeying me."

The punishment my mother meted out was different from that of my father. She put us in a corner with our face to the wall. We had to stay in that position for the rest of the day while the other kids were playing outside. Now this would not have been so bad if it had concluded our punishment for the day. However, when my father returned home from work, he took charge from that point on. I can tell you that when my father was in charge of our punishment, it was not a pleasant experience. Soon after he arrived home later that afternoon, my mother gave him a detailed account of our actions. She told him that we disobeyed her (as we did once before) and left our yard to go down the street and around the corner without her permission. As I am thinking back on this incident, I can recall the words of my mother and father. They would always tell us that you learn your lessons well, as well as being responsible in making the right choices in life." And they would continue, "Because the consequences of your bad choices cannot be blamed on anyone else but you."

My father got very upset after hearing the report my mother gave him on our actions. He talked to us about our attitude and about taking responsibility for our behavior. My father's approach to our disobedience was far different than my mother's. He made it quite clear that the choice we made to disobey our mother called for (words we did not want to hear) "an attitude adjustment." This was one of those times in your life that you really wish your prayers of deliverance could be answered. I can tell you that we knew what was coming next. He concluded his talk by demonstrating a consequence: his belt on our rear ends. It was a very painful lesson that was well learned: listen to the instruction of my mother. I have shared my personal story with you to make this very important point: too often many people suffer bad and profound consequences in life all because of their attitude.

The choices we make in life should be made with good judgment and character. Our attitude plays a very important part in those choices. Our will should be as I previously stated and is worth repeating again: do well in life and by others, knowing that a good attitude will carry you far in life.

The attitude of many people has led them into various negative situations in life. Today, they wish that they could have conducted themselves more appropriately because of the consequences they experienced. Bad attitudes can cause you to suffer consequences that are extreme and beyond your control. The drama that results from bad attitude behavior has resulted in tragedies in the lives of many people, some ending even in death. What positive steps have you taken to correct your attitude?

> To be in denial of your problem
> Will hinder you from self-examination
> And accountability

Our attitude can also cause us to have a haughty spirit and to be high minded. We need to know that this kind of selfish character can also cause some people to be a failure in life. My reason for making this statement is that when life becomes unpleasant for them, they often blame others for their downfall without realizing it is of their own doing. Sad to say, there is an innumerable amount of people who are needlessly suffering hardship in life due to their bad attitude behavior.

A very large number of these people will go through life in denial of their attitude, and will continue to blame others instead of taking responsibility for their actions. Their negative response could be due to hurt and pain from past incidents which they are still harboring. Some people find it easier to blame others for the problems and drama in their lives because they are afraid to take a look at the hurt and pain that is within. People who are placing the blame of their behavior problems on other people will also go as far as to blame God for their bad behavior. They fail to ask the right questions from within, such as: What correctional process am I doing concerning my faults and abnormality? What am I doing to make my life better, inside and out?

The memories of hurt and pain sometimes give rise to anger. It could be from some painful childhood feelings and incidents. Painful memories that are being kept inside can lead to suppressed love. Going through life blaming others always leads to anger, which can get out of control and very often leads you to act out inappropriately. These hidden resentments can make one's life miserable and often those around you. Not recognizing the hidden resentments that they are harboring, it restricts them from expressing themselves in a more positive way.

Those who choose to go through life with the drama and in denial that there is a problem within are denying themselves of peaceful surroundings. Those who choose to be in denial of a drama filled life cause people around them to be uncomfortable. You see, we consciously decide each day whether to be humble, loveable, kind, to do good by people, to be accountable for our actions or to be unreasonable, to be conceited, arrogant, mean, to be unfair in life, to be self-important, to be a know-it-all and the list goes on. These are the choices that we make each day.

People with bad attitudes are often making excuses for their behavior by saying, "I just can't help it; this is who I am. I don't mean anything by it; this is just who I am."

They are in denial of the problem they have by further saying, "There is nothing wrong with me," and, as previously stated, they go through life placing the blame on others. So often when you meet people who have so much drama in their lives, you will also discover that they are hurting inside and their hurt will cause others to hurt. "People, who are hurting, hurt other people."

They find it very difficult to apologize for their misdeeds and to take the necessary steps for change. They think that making excuses for their problems justifies them, but they fail to realize that by taking this approach, the problem will still exist. They do this without looking deep within to really see the hurt and damage they are causing in their lives and character as a person. It is only after one admits that they have a need for change in their attitude behavior, will they seek help for that change. It is after they become aware of the problem that exists that they are willing to take the next step in working through them for change. We should conduct regular self-examinations of ourselves with a willing mind to identify any bad behavior and then seek to make the proper adjustment in attitude.

Many of us fail to realize the wonderful favors of God. The Lord has placed people in our lives as a blessing to us in one way or another and for many of us to be a help through trials and tribulations. These gifts from God could be our parents, other relatives, the person next door, a teacher, co-worker or the homeless person that we walk by on the street. No matter whatever walk of life they are from, we should be able to see the blessing they bring into our lives.

People who are unthankful, unforgiving, unloving, and hard to get along with are going to miss out on the favors of God. We are also going to miss out on the favors of the very people God has given to be a light in our lives. But when we are humble in character, with an attitude of thankfulness, forgiveness, love, meekness, pleasant to talk to, this will attract the good that God has in store for us. It is also true that people are more willing to help someone with a good attitude and they are less likely to help those with a bad attitude.

I think at this point I need to add this warning that is given in the Bible from Gal.6:7: "Be not deceived; God is not mocked: for whatsoever a man soweth, that shall he also reap". Now you would be very surprised if you planted corn in the ground and watermelons came up. So anyone with a self-centered attitude who is evil to his or her friends or says bad things to or about them, should not be surprised if they end up with no friends. It is called the law of life. We must understand that every action has results; what you reap, you will sow. The point here is we should control our tongue and we should relate with people in a productive and caring way.

Our personality should be of great concern to us because it impacts the way we are viewed by other people. Your personality is your quality of being a person, the dynamic character or state of who you are. For anyone who has a good or pleasant personality, you will notice a pattern of good collective character, good behavior, and good emotional and mental traits about them. These people have distinguishing personal characteristics and are socially appealing. Now anyone who has a bad attitude problem can change their behavior but there must be a need within them for change. This, however, must be a deep desire to change not just a superficial feeling. This will come through by seeking the peace of God and having a positive mental attitude.

The important fact that must be understood here is this: we must conduct an honest examination of ourselves to see ourselves as we really are, and have the willingness and desire to make a conscious decision for change. We should then take the responsibility to respond to what we discover in ourselves and make the appropriate change to better our lives. This requires being in tune with ourselves in ways we have overlooked in the past. By taking this approach through the love of God, we are able to overcome the problem by removing self-centeredness and replacing it with self-love and respect for others.

Then God will do greater things in your life. He will bless you both spiritually and naturally. You will be a greater blessing to the people with whom you live, work and worship. Now you have the divine potential within you waiting to blossom into greatness, as God would have you to be, and it all starts with the right attitude and humbleness of heart. There is nothing to hold you back. You will start to see yourself in a new light with an attitude that leads you into faith, hope, peace, joy, in a word… LIFE.

Finally, be charming. It is a wise sort of bewitchment. Let your charm and courtesy capture the goodwill of others, and also their services. It isn't enough to have merit if you don't please others. This is what makes people praise you, and acclaim is the most useful instrument we have for ruling others. You are fortunate if others find you charming which works best when natural gifts are present. Charm leads to benevolence and eventually, universal favor.

Your attitude, after all, "is you." Do you need an attitude adjustment?

Chapter 10

Do You Really Think That You Are a Man?

I feel compelled to write this particular chapter in my book to bring clarity and definition to man's existence. To give justice to this subject, it is important that we understand the origin of man from which he derives his existence. In order for us to come to this knowledge, it is necessary for us to turn our attention to the Bible. It is stated in this holy book that the origin of man was in the predestination of God before the foundation of the world, meaning man was marked out beforehand in the timeless mind of God.

As we begin this discussion, it is important for us to understand the creation of man, as God would have us to know man's origin. Man is a direct product of the hand of God. In Genesis 2:7 it says: "And the Lord formed man of the dust of the ground, and breathed into his nostrils the breath of life; and man became a living soul." This is to be taken at face value because it is the Word of God. Man did not descend from a sub-ape creature (evolution); he was made from the dust of the ground into the image of God being composed of a body, a soul, and spirit.

In the origin of man, we find that God created him in His own image (Gen.1: 27). It is important to note that man was created a Holy human being. As we look into the Word of God, we find that His intended will is for man to be Holy and in his image. We have these words in Ephesians 1:4: "According as He hath chosen us in Him before the foundation of the world, that we should be Holy and without blame before Him in love." This clearly reveals to us that before we ever came into existence, man was predestined by God to live holy. You see, we must understand, as holy men (and women) we are the reflection of God's glory. We reflect His character in love, kindness, patience, forgiveness, and faithfulness.

Again, the point must be made here that before the foundation of the world, man was predestined by God to be in His image and after His likeness. Knowing that we are created in the image of God, we have a duty to live a responsible life unto Him and be a society of men who are accountable unto the Lord. Therefore, man was not created to live a life of dishonor or be irresponsible to the will of God. Man is not here by accident nor is he a by-product. God created man with a purpose in mind. The reason we are here on this earth is because God willed it to be so. For this reason, as men, our desire should be that of holiness and integrity as God wants us to be.

In this day and time in which we live we are truly grateful for all of the social and technological advancements that have been achieved by men and women. The quality of life for mankind has been enhanced such that people are now living longer and healthier lives than in the past. Through the benefit of steady progress in the fields of science and technology, we are now able to achieve on higher levels than in times past. We are realizing achievements today that we only dreamt about in the past. The progress of mankind is remarkable; our advancements into an improved and better quality of life we now enjoy are uncanny.

As previously stated, I am thankful for the dedication and progress we have witnessed as a society. Many necessary achievements and advancements in various fields of technology and medical studies have been realized. So much we have achieved in life as a people are incredible. However, in spite of all the social blessings we now enjoy, my underlying reason for writing this chapter is to address the morality of man. To those men of integrity who are living in purpose, may you continue to be blessed in the name of the Lord. But to the society of those men who do not recognize or accept the purpose God intended for them, it is with extreme urgency I must address this group whom I call the "**poor, careless, society of men**."

As I travel around this country, the facts are the same with regard to so many of our men in society. The morality of man is at an all time low in spite of the availability of books in stores that speak to this concern and the integrity of man. Regretfully, there is a society of men who appear to have no morals nor do they possess any sense of responsibility and accountability. We should consider that there is the book of all books (the bible) that teaches us how to be a better man, a good father, a leader in the community and a productive citizen.

There are many church doors open all over this country that are available to help direct and guide man in his right order and way of life. But, in spite of all of the information and help that is available, many who are so desperately in need of it are not utilizing this guidance. As a result, the morals of man are very low. It is for this reason and so many more that man is not living up to the standards God has intended for him. This society of men seems to have no direction in life; thus, they are unable to set true standards for themselves or for our boys and young men who are looking to them for guidance and example. Our jails and correctional systems have become a revolving door for so many of our men. Many of these men have been conditioned into accepting this as a way of life. As a result, many of our boys are on a downward spiraling path of no true supervision or guidance. Because of this sickness and other socials ills in our society, the morals and standards of man as a whole are not conducive to any good results.

We have a society of young men and boys who are standing on street corners all over this country selling drugs to our women and children. It is becoming common for our women, young and old, to prostitute themselves for drugs and other unworthy causes. They are clueless to the reality of the negative impact of these drugs on family life. In addition, they are equally ignorant of the fact that the drugs they are selling in their community are nothing short of modern day slavery. Many of our youth are glorifying the ghetto life and gangster culture, the modus operandi for "keeping it real." The reality is that there is no glory in living in poverty, going to prison, being killed or contracting a sexually transmitted disease, all frequent consequences of the thug culture. And speaking of sexually transmitted diseases, AIDS remains the leading cause of death among African American women between the ages of 25 and 34. It's the second leading cause of death among black men between the ages of 35-44. In Washington, more than 80 percent (one in 20 residents) of HIV cases are among black people. About 84 percent of all HIV cases in Jackson, Ms. are among black people.

Today, 47 percent of the HIV cases in the United States are African Americans, even though African Americans make up only 13 percent of the population. Too many of our young women are giving birth to babies with mental and physical challenges and other birth defects due to use of drugs and from sexually transmitted diseases. I have some questions: Where are the real men and fathers who will teach our young men and women the difference between right and wrong? Where are the men and fathers who will teach our young men and women how to deal with the conflicts and struggles of life that are sure to occur in their lives? Who will be there to teach them about the adversities of life and how to respond to them in a positive way for good and positive results?

It is a shame indeed to see (this poor, careless society of men) how our males are killing each other daily. Blacks killing blacks and black on black crimes seem to be all too common. Sadly, in so many of our homes mothers are afraid of their own children and grandchildren. Our young men and boys are breaking into our homes stealing, robbing and engaging in many other unlawful and illegal acts. They have become targets for policemen to shoot. Too many of our young children are dying at an early age in so many of our communities. A large number of our young males are killed due to gang violence before they reach the age of nineteen. We are living in scary times. It is mandatory that fathers take responsibility now for their boys and teach them how to be men. Fathers need to be present in the daily lives of their children.

We have a society of males who have no respect for our females. They address them in the most disrespectful way; whether it is in their speech, their music or in public, it all comes out the same. These immoral males have become a disgrace to society and they compound the issue by acting so disrespectful towards our females. It is without a doubt very shameful the way in which these men address our women with such degrading names using the filthiest language. This conflicts with the purpose for which they were created by God. God created the woman to be man's glory but where are the men to receive them as such?

It pains me to witness this moral decline in our society. It is mandatory that our men get back to treating our mothers, sisters, daughters and other women in our community with the utmost love and respect that they all deserve. If there ever is a time man should be responsive to this clamor for integrity, it is now. We need more and more men to set high standards for our young men. This is not the time for men to be insensitive to the cry for a return to good morals and responsibility; the call is being made on so many of our street corners and in our communities. Too many of our young children idolize drug pushers and gang bangers as heroes. These are the people that they look up to with blind admiration. Sadly, in this area of social responsibility men have fallen short from the intended will of God.

Many males go out in public dressed indecently with their trousers way down below their waist unnecessarily revealing their underwear. You will find that many of them are between 30 and 40 years old—male adults who should be the ones setting a good example for our young children. Too many of these men in this poor careless society of males father babies but refuse to get a job to provide for them. To reiterate, a lack of good morals in this society is resulting in unresponsiveness to the call for integrity. The call is being made each and every day: "Will the real men and fathers please stand and take your rightful place?" When men's hearts and desires become focused on God's purpose for them, they will do the right thing and they can make a difference in the lives of their children.

It is deplorable to see in this poor, careless society of males those who produce babies but reject the responsibilities of fatherhood. They fail to understand that producing a child does not make them a man in the process nor does it automatically make them a father. Many of these males are very immature in their thoughts and actions. Their behaviors reflect self-centeredness and a total lack of priorities. It is of more concern and importance to them to buy expensive wheels for their cars than it is to pay child support for the babies they have produced. They place a higher value on the concern and care of their cars than taking the responsibility to provide for their children. A real man accepts responsibility to provide the necessary care for the baby he has fathered. He places a higher value and importance on the care and well being of his child than on the wheels of his car or any other recreational activity.

A real father provides loving care for his children; he is the present in their lives as much as possible surrounding them with love, giving them proper guidance and supervision. He is a man of responsibility; he is accountable to his children by instilling in them a sense of excellence. Real men and fathers teach their boys how to become men and bring them into the knowledge of Christ. I believe that one of the most important duties of a father is taking his children to church to worship and thank the Lord for their blessings.

If we are truly honest with ourselves, we would admit that too many of our fathers are missing in action, too many of our fathers have gone AWOL. They are missing from the lives of their children and from their homes. We have too many fathers who have abandoned their responsibility; they are acting like boys rather than men. This is truer in the African American family than any other family in America. Over half of all black children live in single family homes. Research shows that children who grow up without a father in the home are five times more likely to live in poverty and commit crime. They are nine times more likely to drop out of school and twenty times more likely to end up in prison. They are more likely to have behavior problems, run away from home or become teen parents. We are called to recognize how critical the father is to the character development of the family.

In communities across this nation our young children have to contend with such influences as gangs, violence, drugs and other social ills on a daily basis. The temptations of these bad influences are extremely difficult for these young minds to contend with, and this challenge is compounded when there is no foundational parental care and supervision from the father. Throughout this nation we have many "baby daddies," but what we need are real men who will step up to the plate and be responsible fathers to their children. More than 60 percent of all African American children are growing up in homes without fathers. It takes much prayer and time than ever before in this day and season for fathers to be there for our sons (and daughters) giving them proper guidance and supervision. It is so important to be there in their early years as they develop in our presence into manhood (and womanhood).

In the Bible you find these instructions (Proverbs: 22-6): "Train up a child in the way he should go; and when he is old, he will not depart from it." I cannot stress this fact enough; it is so important that we be there for our children to teach and educate them about life and the Lord. Thereby, we are setting good standards for them to live by. If there is no road map to the destination, then the traveler will make some bad turns in the roads of life along the way, some of which could be lethal (deadly). Now I do understand it is not always easy and, depending on what side of the track you are from, it could be even more difficult for you than the next person. But every man is going to encounter pitfalls and challenges along the way; the difference is the man of integrity will confront them in a positive way and keep moving forward. We are going to make some mistakes at times but a real man can and will acknowledge them and keep trying harder to do better. You see, the road map he is designing is major.

As a little boy, I felt a great sense of pride seeing my father going to work each day to provide for the family. It was a wonderful feeling. It is important to have a father functioning in the home because it gives a child a deep sense of security. I also remember those weekends when my father would be outside working around the house. My brothers and I would be there working alongside my dad while my mother would be working inside with my sisters. We would help him as he cut the grass and repainted the sheds that he had built to store his tools and other equipment. When the truck or cars were not running well, we would help our dad fix them and get them back in working order. We looked forward to doing so many things as a family. Then he and my mom would always talk to us about being responsible young men, accountable for our actions and making the right choices in life.

We did not know it at the time but they were designing a road map of life for us. My father would tell us that one day we would become fathers with our own families and that it would be our job as responsible parents to teach and guide our children in the right direction. He encouraged my mother to teach her sons how to cook; my mother also felt this was necessary in case one of our wives became sick and was unable to care for her self or the children. There were so many important things that she taught us such as to always be respectable toward women, pull the chair out for a lady to sit in, open the door for them to enter, ladies are first, help her with her coat, etc. They would tell us that one day we will be married and parents of our own children and that we must be responsible parents, teaching them responsibility and respect. They also emphasized taking our family to church as we are bringing them up and into the knowledge of Christ. What a road map of life!!! And for this I will be forever grateful.

We can no longer afford to sit idly by or stand on the sidelines of life and watch with resentment and displeasure while the demise of this part of our society of males continues. In many of our cities the dropout rate for males in high schools is reaching an all time high and this national problem is now seeping into our middle schools. Our children in middle school are being exposed to the uses and selling of drugs; they are facing dangerous challenges and are being forced to grow up and deal with them at a much earlier age. They are struggling with such major social issues and are encountering temptations no child should have to contend with. These obstacles and hindrances that confront our children on a daily basis are very destructive. They hinder their well-being, give rise to educational concerns, and may have a negative impact on their future.

This is a critical situation! An urgent plea is being made to men and fathers: Will you please come and take your rightful place in society? The blood of our sons and daughters are crying out from the earth, can you hear their cry? Do you hear the despairing cry of the mothers for our sons and daughters? Our destitute women and children are sleeping in the streets of our cities, abandoned cars, and shelters for the homeless, can you see their needs? The average number of African-American males in this country who are in college is 864,000 while about 802,000 are behind bars in a penitentiary or some other correctional institution. So come now, men and fathers, let us sit at the table of brotherhood that we may reason together. **A mind is a terrible thing to waste.**

When the fathers are away, the children will play, but sad to say, many of our children are playing dead-end games that prove to be destructive and do not have a happy ending, games that will consume them. Too many fathers have failed to take their role seriously as leaders of their families. Consequently, many of our children are falling into the same trap because of the lack of positive leadership. It is alarming to see so many of our sons lacking direction and guidance in their lives because of absent fathers. The social consequences are devastating for this poor, careless society of men who have taken a back seat to life and will not respond to the call for responsibility.

Live your life with purpose
and integrity.

My grandfather was well known and highly respected in the city in which he lived. He was Chairman of the deacon board at the church he attended and was a mason in which he served as a high-ranking leader in that fraternal order. (My understanding is very limited in their degree of that fraternal order). My grandfather was loved by many people. He had a gift for helping people who came from far and wide seeking his assistance to alleviate their worries and concerns. Their needs ranged from a court case or a discrepancy with another to financial or family matters. The reason I am mentioning my grandfather is because he truly lived a life of purpose and integrity. At the time of his death, he testified: "I have fulfilled my purpose here in this life." I truly loved and respected my grandfather because he was a great man. There is a quotation he was known for saying that will always be with me and it is this: **"A man is not a man in his age alone, but also the person of character he develops into and of accountability."** You see, we men have the responsibility to be men and to return to the purpose, which God had intended for us. I pray that in your reading of this book you will seek and find your purpose in life.

God Himself, the creator of all mankind, is making the call for men to return unto Him and start living a life that is honorable and accountable to Him. Ps.100: 3 states: "Know ye that the Lord He is God: it is He that hath made us, and not we ourselves; we are his people, and the sheep of his pasture." This quote summarizes for us that He has made us and we are his people. Thereby He is giving us clear understanding that we belong to the Lord and He is calling men back to purpose. There is a matter at hand that needs to be taken care of and as of now we are missing the goal. We must strive to be

Elder G. E. Johnson

what God had intended for us in fulfilling our purpose here on earth.

Responsibility and accountability are two words I have used often in the writing of this book. If men would take heed and consider the meaning and the importance of these two words in their truest form, they will recognize the urgent need for change. They will then have a willing mind to align their lives in accordance with the Word of God. Submitting to the Word of God would make their lives more meaningful.

I played football for my high school team. I loved playing the game and was very good at it. The position I played on the team was a running back. In my last year in high school, we lost a game to a team that had not won a game all season. We were very upset about the loss and did not handle our emotions well. That night some of the guys decided to break some of the windows at the school before getting on the bus to return home. Now my mother would always tell my brothers and me that if we should ever find ourselves in the company of boys who are trying to get into trouble we should distance ourselves immediately and come home. I remembered my mother's words, but I failed to heed them. I made the decision not to break any windows at the school, but had chosen to remain in their company. My reason for staying in their company while they carried out the destruction was that I did not want these guys to think I was chicken or a mommy's boy. I thought to myself, "After all, I am old enough now to make my own decision as to whether to go or stay here in the company of my teammates."

To my surprise, the very next day the police officers came through our neighborhood and arrested the boys who had broken the school windows along with all of those "who were connected" with the vandalism. The next thing that surprised me was the willingness of my mother for the officers to arrest me after she had discovered I had participated in the vandalism. She believed this would help me to understand what she was trying to tell me. We were all taken to jail. That very same day each of those boys' parents came and got them out of jail. I was also anticipating that my mother would come and get me out but, to my surprise, she did not. She left me in jail over the weekend to teach me a lesson that I could have learned just by listening to her. I was very fearful and terrified because this was my first time in jail and I was crying and pleading for my mother to come and get me out, but she would not.

My mother waited until just before school began on Monday morning to come and get me out of jail. She would not let the officers release me until she had disciplined me and talked with me about the consequences of my bad decision. I must say to you, I was so very emotionally gratified and relieved to see my mother. I was ready to listen with respect and obedience to her teachings and instructions. As I look back on that experience, I realize that I learned a life lesson. I am blessed to be the person I am today, a man of integrity and holiness, because of the consistent guidance and appropriate consequences I received from my parents. I know that I am better off today because my mother did not come to get me out right away, and it did me much good to have time to reflect on my wrong actions. She did not think it would have benefited me to get me out immediately as my friends' parents did without any disciplinary action. Later on, it was very obvious that she was right—most of my friends, except for one, continued to live irresponsible lives. Let us be men and live our lives accountable, responsible and in admiration of the Lord.

It is stated in Isaiah 43: 6-7: " I will say to the north, give up; and to the south, keep not back; bring my sons from far, and my daughters from the end of the earth; Even every one that is called by my name; for I have created him for my glory, I have formed him; yea, I have made him." Know who you are, my friend: a child of God. It is God who has made you, and you depend on Him for your very existence here on earth. The question that comes to mind is this: What is the purpose for your existence here on earth? If you really think about it, you will come to learn that you were not created to be destructive to yourself or others nor were you created to live an irresponsible life. Could it be that you are fearful, lost and in need of direction? Return to Him who created you and He will guide you in the direction that He has destined for you.

As I have stated in chapter 6, the Bible is not an option. It is the Word of God, the inspired and infallible Word of God. The Bible is not a book that we can read and just select those things we like and decide to live by, or put aside those things we do not like. To have a relationship with God and live in His presence, we must live according to His whole Word.

There is a verse in the Bible I would like to present to you; it is Deuteronomy 30:19: "I call heaven and earth to record this day against you, that I have set before you life and death, blessing and cursing: therefore choose life, that both thou and thy seed may live." When you are living a careless, irresponsible life, you are living a meaningless, dead-end life. This is not the life God intended for you to live. Choose to live according to his Word and you will fulfill the purpose for which the Lord has created you. I strongly encourage you to get to know the Lord and live in the peace, which comes with a relationship with Him. It starts with seeking Jesus Christ as your Lord and Savior, then having a good, positive attitude, living a responsible life, and being accountable unto the Lord. Let this day be the day you start anew. MAKE THE RIGHT CHOICE: CHOOSE GOD.

Of Elder G. E. Johnson

Names are very important in Scripture; a name often represents the nature, character, attributes, and destiny of a person.

God's name Yahweh, for example, point of the fact; God is self-existent "I am who I am" "I will be who I will be."

The name "Jesus" means = "Yahweh is salvation" and points to the Lord's role as savior of humankind.

The title "Christ" reveals that Jesus is the anointed Messiah. Other names and titles of Christ reveal various aspects of his person and work.

The Holy Spirit is a member of the God head who indwells the believers and helps us in every area of our lives the bible call him the paraklete, which is often translated as comforter, counselor, helper, or advocate.

In the above passage the Holy Spirit is manifest in a manner represented by two emblems: wind and fire. At various places in the old and new Testament, the Spirit also is characterized

Elder G. E. Johnson

as a dove, dew, river, and oil. All these images give us valuable insights into the ministry of the third member of the Trinity.

A wind removes what is stale and can also bring comforter. A breath, which is a type of wind, brings life. A fire purifier and can spread rather quickly. A dove is a clean bird and often represents purity and peace. Dew is normally associated with the morning (i.e., new beginnings after a dark night of despair). Rivers quench thirst and bring refreshment. Finally oil provides fuel and revitalizes cracked places. The Holy Spirit is like all these emblems. He cleanses, enables, invigorates, restores, and refreshes. He is important the very life of God into our spirit.